BASIC JUDAISM FOR YOUNG PEOPLE: **TORAH**

BASIC JUDAISM
FOR YOUNG PEOPLE

VOLUME TWO

TORAH

NAOMI PASACHOFF, PH.D.

BEHRMAN HOUSE, INC., PUBLISHERS

WEST ORANGE, NEW JERSEY

To my daughters, Eloise and Deborah,
and to my husband, Jay

Designer: Martin Lubin/Betty Binns Graphics
Artists: Tony Chen and Jody Wheeler
Project editor: Geoffrey Horn

The editor and publisher gratefully acknowledge the cooperation of the fol-
lowing sources of photographs for this book:

Bill Aron Photography, 2, 10, 59, 73, 92–93; Bill Aron/Art Resource, 118; Mi-
cha Bar-Am/Magnum, 32, 84; Bettmann Archive, 27, 129, 132; Rick Fried-
man/Black Star, 108; D. W. Funt/Art Resource, 145; Hebrew Union
College–Skirball Museum, 8, 55 (all except top row right and second row
center), 86 (top), 98 (bottom); Jewish Museum/Art Resource, 20, 86 (bottom), 116; Paolo Koch/Photo Researchers, 104; Vernon Merritt III/Black Star,
21; James Nachtwey/Black Star, 142; Richard Nowitz/Black Star, 62; Jay M.
Pasachoff, 11, 64–65, 68, 88, 110, 119, 122; Gail Rubin/Photo Researchers,
18–19; Israel Ministry of Tourism, 43; Israel Museum, Jerusalem, 98 (top);
Scala/Art Resource, 46; Ted Spiegel/Black Star, 38, 52, 138–39; Tel Aviv
Museum, 81; UAHC Synagogue Art and Architecture Library, 35, 40, 48–49,
55 (top row right and second row center), 90, 96, 98, 99; United Jewish Appeal, 124, 134–35.

Library of Congress Cataloging-in-Publication Data

Pasachoff, Naomi E.
        Basic Judaism for young people.

        "Artists: Tony Chen and Jody Wheeler"—Vol. 2, p.
        Includes index.
        Contents: —v. 2. Torah.
        1. Judaism—Juvenile literature. [1. Judaism—
Dictionaries] I. Chen, Tony, ill. II. Wheeler, Jody,
ill. III. Title.
BM573.P37 1986   296   86-1214
ISBN 0-87441-424-5 (v. 2)

CONTENTS

FOREWORD:
TO THE TEACHER

The Torah is the first word of God, not the last. It does not end with Deuteronomy or with the Second Book of Chronicles. The Torah is the major thrust of an ongoing tradition of text and commentary, of law and responsa, of tales and parables reaching into our own day. In this broadest sense, the culture of Torah cannot be closed because it lives as long as the Jewish people does.

The complexity and continuity of Jewish sacred culture are illustrated in this second of Naomi Pasachoff's more than basic books of Judaism for young people. May I suggest to the teacher some of the subthemes that run through this *Torah* volume.

Jewish intellectuality is multifaceted. Rabbi Pinḥas of Koretz had a burning desire to be a תַּלְמִיד־חָכָם, a scholar. But the people of his village kept coming to him with personal questions that interrupted his studies. In desperation he prayed that no one should approach him—that he should be left alone, free to delve into the labyrinthine subtleties of Torah. And his prayer was granted. During the Days of Awe no one approached him, and after Yom Kippur no one would help him build his Sukkah, nor would any of the villagers visit him there. Rabbi Pinḥas invited the patriarchs into his Sukkah in accordance with the custom of אֻשְׁפִּיזִין (guests), but they all declined, saying, "We do not enter a home where our children are unwelcome." Alone with his sacred books, Rabbi Pinḥas now prayed for his earlier prayer to be annulled. For what is the meaning of learning if it leads to isolation from our fellow human beings?

Our sages taught that we must not simply know Torah but live Torah. We must seek not theoretical knowledge of Torah but wisdom that is acted out in living with others. "He whose wisdom exceeds his deeds, to what is he like? To a tree whose branches are many but whose roots are few; and the wind comes and plucks it up and overturns it upon its face" (Pirke Avot 3:22). Study alone is not sufficient for the good life, for Jewish intellectuality must be linked to moral and spiritual goals. As the Talmud in Avodah Zarah points out sharply, "He who only studies Torah is considered as one who has no God."

No human being is above criticism, but each person has the power to seek justice and renew Creation. Another subtheme running through the text is that the Torah and commentaries treat men and women of power in an extraordinarily candid way. No king, prince, priest, or prophet is above criticism. The Navi Nathan confronts no less a figure than King David with two resounding Hebrew words that pierce the false armor of his rationalization: אַתָּה הָאִישׁ, "Thou art the man" (Samuel 12:7).

More than prophetic candor is involved in such a confrontation. The Biblical and rabbinic traditions struggle against the deification of humanity, the surrender to monarchs and holy men as if they were gods. In the eyes of some rabbinic commentators, Sarah's and Abraham's behavior toward Hagar and Ishmael is far from exemplary, and the favoritism shown by Rebecca and Isaac bears bitter fruit. Jacob's deception of Isaac, the High Priest Aaron's appeasement of the mob clamoring for the golden calf, Moses' expression of anger and pride in striking the rock for water—all illustrate the limitations of flesh and blood. The reflective conclusion of Ecclesiastes (7:20) resonates in the Jewish consciousness: "There is no just person on earth who does good and does not sin."

Flawed as human beings are, they alone have the power to challenge sovereign powers who act unjustly. When God, resolving not to hide from Abraham his intention "to do righteousness and justice" (Genesis 18:19), discloses that Sodom and Gomorrah are to be destroyed, the patriarch is emboldened to demand that the Judge of all earth act justly, not punishing the innocent along with the wicked. Between God and Abraham stands a moral covenant: one law on earth as in heaven. The children of the covenant are to be kept from the extremes of self-deification and self-deprecation, both of which may lead to passivity. Rather, the covenant calls upon errant humanity to mend the broken vessels of this world and to take part in the daily renewal of Creation.

Torah has many faces. The alphabetically arranged table of contents of our book includes Aggadah and Halachah, Minhag as well as Tanach. The reason for such breadth is that Torah is more than a body of scripture. Torah mirrors the astounding interaction of a living people with its everchanging environment. It has a life of its own and is seen differently by each generation. "The Torah has seventy faces," the sages said. "Turn it around and around, for everything is in it."

The literal-minded instructor may ask such questions as "How could so many animals fit into an ark?" or "How can a serpent speak?" or "How many rungs were on Jacob's ladder?" The rabbinic, philosophic, and mystical traditions, however, recognize that there is much more to the text than meets the literalist's eye. As the Zohar explains, if the Torah comes merely to tell us a piece of history and nothing more, it can hold no sacred truths. "Now if it is not dignified for a king of flesh and blood to engage in common talk, much less write it down, is it conceivable that the most high King, the Holy One, blessed be He, was short of sacred subjects to fill the Torah? Did He have to collect such commonplace topics as the anecdotes of Esau and of Hagar, Laban's talks to Jacob, the words of Balaam and his ass, those of Balak and of Zimri and suchlike, and make of them a Torah?"

To seek out the inner meaning of Torah, a teacher of Judaism should search the narration with a midrashic eye. What meaning does the Noah story hold for our people? How does the Haftarah of Noah reveal the way a much later rabbinic generation viewed the flood and the saving remnant? The way the teacher frames the question conditions the way the student responds to the text. Answers to questions that ask *who, when, where*, and *how* are easier to grade, but answers to questions of *why* and *what for* allow the Bible to take on new significance.

To ask which siblings in the Bible were twins, for example, calls for an act of memory; to speculate about the Torah's motives for noting the twinship of Jacob and Esau encourages a wider and deeper view of the narrative. Such an inquiry may reveal another dimension to Jacob's wrestling with the "angel" alone, at night, at the ford of the Jabbok, before his encounter with the aggrieved Esau. Is the mysterious stranger the shadow twin side of Jacob, or what modern people call conscience? Is this struggle a vision, or is it a physical encounter? Is the limping Jacob a traumatized figure? And if so, is his trauma a self-inflicted punishment, a blow to repay the injury done to Esau and Isaac?

The Bible is neither a book of legends nor an objective account of history. Nor is it a scientific document. Rather, it is an interpretation of the genesis, development, and growing self-awareness of a people in its search for sacred meaning. For Jews it is a family album showing who we are and what we are yet to become. The patriarchs and matriarchs are our family, our מִשְׁפָּחָה. We are drawn to understand them — their character, struggles, and ideals — because they help us understand our spiritual roots. These tales of sibling rivalry and reconciliation, of the formulation of our people and the disclosure of God's ways, of laws and statutes discovered and revealed, continue to inform our lives today. Tallit,

Tefillin, Mezuzah, Torah, Haftarah, Ner Tamid, Brit, Pidyon HaBen, Ketubah and Get, Shabbat and festivals, Hallel and prayers — all are derived and embellished from the inexhaustible source, the sacred text out of which are woven commentaries, basic attitudes, and ways of moral, ritual, and liturgical behavior.

Torah is not a story about an ancient people. Torah is not about "them" but about us, our children, and our children's children. It is an intergenerational sacred text that forms the character of what we as Jews hold in common.

RABBI HAROLD M. SCHULWEIS

PREFACE:
TO THE STUDENT

Although this book is about Torah, it is not on a scroll, and you don't unroll it. But you do have to "unfold" its ideas and have fun with them in order to enjoy it fully.

In some ways, our book is like a dictionary. But this is a very special kind of dictionary — a dictionary of words and ideas that tell what it means to be Jewish. The book has many beginnings, and each chapter is a fresh start.

We have gathered in this book some of the favorite ideas of the Jewish people. We are proud to have included so much special information — ways of finding out when things happened in history and who the important people were, along with the extra tidbits of information that make learning more enjoyable.

Most of all, we treasure the many stories our people have told about what it's like to be Jewish. We hope that you have a good time reading these stories, and that you enjoy being part of the Jewish tradition.

Best wishes,

RABBI WILLIAM CUTTER

The Alef-Bet   אָלֶף בֵּית

ENGLISH SOUND	ENGLISH NAME	NUMBER VALUE	HEBREW NAME	LETTER
—	alef	1	אָלֶף	א
b	bet	2	בֵּית	בּ
v	vet		בֵית	ב
g	gimmel	3	גִּמֶל	ג
d	dalet	4	דָּלֶת	ד
h	hay	5	הֵא	ה
v	vav	6	וָו	ו
z	zayin	7	זַיִן	ז
ḥ	ḥet	8	חֵית	ח
t	tet	9	טֵית	ט
y	yod	10	יוֹד	י
k	kaf	20	כָּף	כּ
ḥ	chaf		כָף	כ
ḥ	final chaf		כָף סוֹפִית	ך
l	lamed	30	לָמֶד	ל
m	mem	40	מֵם	מ
m	final mem		מֵם סוֹפִית	ם
n	nun	50	נוּן	נ
n	final nun		נוּן סוֹפִית	ן
s	samech	60	סָמֶך	ס
—	ayin	70	עַיִן	ע
p	pay	80	פֵּא	פּ
f	fay		פֵא	פ
f	final fay		פֵא סוֹפִית	ף
ts, tz	tzadee	90	צָדִי	צ
ts, tz	final tzadee		צָדִי סוֹפִית	ץ
k	kof	100	קוֹף	ק
r	resh	200	רֵישׁ	ר
sh	shin	300	שִׁין	שׁ
s	sin		שִׂין	שׂ
t	tav	400	תָּו	תּ
t	tav		תָו	ת

Note: The ḥ sound is variously represented in English as ch, h, ḥ, or kh (e.g., **Ch**anukah or **Ḥ**anukkah, **ch**allah or **ḥ**allah, hala**ch**ah or hala**kh**ah).

INTRODUCTION:
THE TORAH AND THE ALEF-BET

One of the first things you learned when you began your Jewish education was the alef-bet, the Hebrew alphabet. Your teachers taught you the alef-bet with the hope that by the time you reached Bar or Bat Mitzvah age, you would be able to read Torah in Hebrew.

The subject of this book is Torah. In the pages that follow, many different topics related to Torah are arranged in their Hebrew alphabetical order, from alef to tav, א to ת.

If you write out the twenty-two letters of the alef-bet and include in their places the five final letters (chaf, mem, nun, fay, tzadee), you will see that there are twenty-seven letters in all. The first letter, of course, is alef, and the last, of course, is tav. The middle letter, surrounded by thirteen others on each side, is mem. These three letters together—alef, mem, tav—spell out the Hebrew word for "truth," אֱמֶת. The Torah is often called "Torat emet"—the Torah of truth. You may even know a song based on these words.

Ever since the Torah was given to our ancestors, people have studied it carefully to find the "truths" in it. In this book you will read about the Aggadah (אַגָּדָה), the Midrash (מִדְרָשׁ), and the Talmud (תַּלְמוּד), all of which came from studies to uncover the Torah's truths.

One of the first parts of the Torah that our ancestors received was the Ten Commandments (Aseret HaDibrot). The first word of the Ten Commandments begins with an alef. After the Bible itself, the most basic book in Jewish life is the Talmud. The Talmud has two parts, the Mishnah and the Gemara. The first word of the Mishnah begins with a mem, and the first word of the Gemara begins with a tav. The alef from the beginning of the Ten Commandments, the mem from the beginning of the Mishnah, and the tav from the beginning of the Gemara together spell אֱמֶת, truth.

The story of Creation in the Torah teaches us a lesson about truth. The first three words of the Torah are: "In the beginning, God created (בְּרֵאשִׁית בָּרָא אֱלֹהִים)." Notice the last letters of these three words: tav, alef, mem. These are the letters of the word emet, but the letters are scrambled.

After the six days of Creation came the first Shabbat. The Torah says God rested on the seventh day, after completing the Creation that "God created to make":

בָּרָא אֱלֹהִים לַעֲשׂוֹת.

What does the Torah mean when it repeats the idea of Creation with the words "to make"? These words may mean that God created an unfinished world. It is the job of people to help God complete His work. Notice that the final letters of בָּרָא אֱלֹהִים לַעֲשׂוֹת — alef, mem, tav — are in the correct order to spell אֱמֶת. Truth—אֱמֶת—in one form or another keeps appearing in the Torah.

You study the letters of the alef-bet not only to form Hebrew words but also to uncover ancient truths.

אַגָּדָה

AGGADAH
ä·gä·dä′

Aggadah is Hebrew for "narration" or "telling a story." The subject matter of Aggadah ranges from science to fables, from philosophy to stories about Biblical and historical figures.

The word "Aggadah" is related to "Haggadah," the Passover story.

CHAPTER ONE

Rabbi Abbahu and Rabbi Ḥiyya bar Abba once came to the same town to give sermons. Rabbi Abbahu based his sermon on Aggadah. Rabbi Ḥiyya, on the other hand, based his sermon on Halachah, which is Jewish law. A huge audience gathered to hear Rabbi Abbahu's talk, while only a very few scholars attended Rabbi Ḥiyya's talk.

After completing their sermons, the two rabbis met. Rabbi Ḥiyya felt discouraged that so few people had attended his talk while so many had gone to hear Rabbi Abbahu. To console him, Rabbi Abbahu said, "My friend, you know that studies of Halachah appeal mainly to scholars, while Aggadah appeals to all people. You with your sermon based on Halachah are like a merchant who sells precious jewels. Only a few people need and appreciate such things. I, on the other hand, with my sermon based on Aggadah, am like a merchant who sells inexpensive shoes, which are bought and needed by most people."

In this chapter, you will learn how stories about our great rabbis in the Aggadah teach us Jewish ideas about very difficult questions. In the first section, a story about Rabban Gamaliel teaches us about the Jewish belief in God. In the second section, a story about Beruriah and her husband, Rabbi Meir, tries to explain death. Each story is an example of the legends of the Aggadah.

CHAPTER SUMMARY

Lesson 1: The Aggadah teaches us that God is everywhere we look for Him.

Lesson 2: The Aggadah helps us understand the meaning of life and death.

Aggadah and God

A non-Jew once asked Rabbi Joshua ben Karḥa why God spoke to Moses from a lowly thorn bush. Rabbi Joshua said to him, "You would ask me the same question no matter from where God chose to address Moses. But all the same, I have

SEE FOR YOURSELF

The story of Rabbi Abbahu and Rabbi Ḥiyya appears in the Talmud at Sotah 40a. The Talmud (Sanhedrin 39a) is also the source of the story of how Rabban Gamaliel defended God.

◁ Rabban Gamaliel used the example of sunlight to show how God could be in many places at the same time.

an answer for you. God spoke to Moses from the thorn bush
to teach you that God exists everywhere, even in a thorn
bush." Rabbi Joshua was not the only rabbi about whose defense of Judaism the Aggadah tells us. Ask yourself as you
read on:

How did Rabban Gamaliel come to the defense of God?

HOW RABBAN GAMALIEL DEFENDED GOD

Rabban Gamaliel was the head of a Jewish court called the
Sanhedrin. The person who held this important position had
the title "Rabban" rather than simply "Rabbi."

A non-Jew once came to Rabban Gamaliel with the following challenge: "I know that one of the Psalms in your
Torah claims that God's presence can be found in every congregation that studies the Torah. How can you make such a
claim? How can God be in so many places?"

Instead of answering directly, Rabban Gamaliel called the
non-Jew's servant and asked him to open the window. When
the servant had done so, Gamaliel lightly tapped him on the
neck. "Why did you permit the sun to enter this house?"
Gamaliel asked him.

"What choice did I have, Rabbi?" answered the servant.
"The sun shines all over the world."

Turning now to the master, Rabban Gamaliel said, "Your
servant has answered your question for me. If the sun, which
is only one of God's servants, can be all over the world at the
same time, how much more so is that true of God's presence."

Another day, Rabban Gamaliel was asked to defend God
against a different charge. "Your God is a thief," said a non-
Jew. "In the Book of Genesis it says that God caused Adam
to fall asleep so that He could take one of his ribs to make a
woman out of it."

This time, the non-Jew's daughter heard the challenge
and rose to the defense. "A thief came to our house one night
and took our silver goblet. In its place the thief left a golden
one."

Beruriah consoled her husband, Rabbi Meir, on the
death of their children by
comparing the two boys to a
borrowed treasure.

"I wish such a thief would come to my house regularly," said her father.

The young woman then said, "You have answered your own challenge against God. Wasn't the first man as pleased to exchange a rib for a wife as you would be to exchange a silver goblet for a gold one?"

REVIEW IT

1. What Aggadah explains how God's presence can be everywhere at the same time?

2. What Aggadah defends God for taking part of Adam's body?

3. Which Aggadah of the two do you think more clearly describes God's power? Be prepared to defend your choice.

An Aggadah about mourning

The Aggadah helps us understand Jewish ideas about many difficult questions, including the meaning of life and death. After you read the following Aggadah, you should be able to answer this:

Why did Beruriah tell her husband that she had to return a borrowed treasure to its owner?

HOW BERURIAH CONSOLED RABBI MEIR

It was Shabbat afternoon, and as usual Rabbi Meir was at the synagogue, studying. But while he was gone, a terrible thing happened at his home. His two sons, whom he dearly loved, died of plague.

Beruriah, the boys' mother, spread a linen cloth over their bodies. Then she spent the afternoon alone in her room, crying over the loss of her two children. As evening approached, she tried to compose herself. She thought about how she could best break the news to her husband when he returned from his studies.

As three stars appeared in the night sky, Rabbi Meir returned home from the synagogue. He embraced Beruriah and immediately asked to see their sons. "They have gone to study," she told him.

"That's strange," said Rabbi Meir. "I didn't see them at the synagogue."

Beruriah handed Rabbi Meir a twisted candle, a spice box, and a wine cup. Rabbi Meir used these items to perform the Havdalah ceremony that separates Shabbat from the workweek. Then again he asked her, "Where have the boys gone?" She answered, "They went for a visit, and have now returned."

She led Rabbi Meir to the dining room table, where he made the blessing over the food. As they ate, she said to him, "Let me ask you a question. Some time ago, a man came to me and gave me a treasure to keep for him. He came again today and asked me to return the treasure to him. What shall I do?"

Rabbi Meir answered, "There should be no question at all in your mind. Of course you must return the treasure to its rightful owner."

Beruriah then took Rabbi Meir's hand and led him to the boys' bedroom. When she removed the cloth that covered their bodies, Rabbi Meir began to cry.

His wife put her arms around him and said, "Didn't you just tell me that I must return the treasure to the man who asked me to keep it for him? The Lord has given, the Lord has taken away. Blessed be the name of the Lord."

Oil lamps rather than candles were used for lighting during the time of the rabbis. This oil lamp filler, made of terracotta, is more than 2000 years old.

REVIEW IT

1. Beruriah compared her sons to (a) sunlight, (b) twin thorn bushes, (c) a borrowed treasure.

2. What might the Aggadah mean when it says that people are on loan from God?

3. Why have we Jews used stories to answer difficult questions?

הֲלָכָה

HALACHAH
hä · lä · ḥä'

Jewish law is called **Halachah.** Halachah makes Judaism a distinctive religion. Although Halachah is based on the Torah, Halachah is continually changing along with the conditions of Jewish life.

Scholars think that the word הֲלָכָה comes from the Hebrew word meaning "to walk," הָלַךְ. Halachah teaches us which path to walk upon.

Halachah teaches us which path to walk upon.

9

Facing page: a young boy examines a Torah scroll. Above: how many letters with crowns do you see in this close-up?

Thirteen letters of the alef-bet have their tops decorated with crowns every time they appear in the Torah. Seven letters (שׁ עׁ זׁ טׁ גׁ צׁ) each have three crown strokes, and six letters (ב ד כ ח י ה) have one. A legend says that when Moses went to the top of Mount Sinai to receive the Torah, he found God providing crowns for these letters. "Why are you going to all this bother?" asked Moses.

"Many generations from now," said God, "there will live a man who will study these crowns to explain Halachah."

"Let me see this man," said Moses.

A moment later, Moses found himself in a classroom filled with scholars. Taking a seat at the end of the ninth row, Moses listened carefully to their discussion. Try as he might, he could not understand the topic they were discussing.

Suddenly, Moses heard Rabbi Akiba explain to one of the younger scholars how he had arrived at a conclusion. "This Halachah was handed down by Moses from Mount Sinai," said Rabbi Akiba.

Moses was very pleased by what he had witnessed. He was not upset that he couldn't understand Rabbi Akiba's interpretation of Halachah, even though Rabbi Akiba had based that interpretation on Moses' own words. Moses understood that change is a basic part of life. He knew that if the Torah is to guide Jewish life, the Halachah based on the Torah must be open to change, too.

The idea about the crowns may be a bit exaggerated, but the legend is important because it emphasizes the need for change through interpretation.

In this chapter, you will learn how Halachah helps Jews observe the Torah's commandments. You will also learn that because God gave the Torah to people, Halachah is determined by people, as democratically as possible.

CHAPTER SUMMARY

Lesson 1: Halachah explains in detail how to observe the Torah's commandments.

Lesson 2: Halachah is a guide for every generation.

Halachah explains the details of observance

In describing the observance of Yom Kippur, the Torah says nothing about fasting. The Torah simply says, "and you shall afflict your souls." If not for Halachah, everyone who read the Torah could make up his or her own interpretation of what exactly the Torah means by that statement. Does it mean, for example, that we should whip ourselves until we bleed? As you read about how Halachah explains the details of Yom Kippur observance, ask yourself:

How does Halachah make it possible for Jews to observe the Torah's Mitzvot in the same way?

HALACHAH FOR YOM KIPPUR OBSERVANCE

According to Halachah, "and you shall afflict your souls" refers to several specific ways of controlling our appetites.

Eating   Halachah explains that, beginning with Bar and Bat Mitzvah age, Jews are required to fast from before sundown on Yom Kippur eve until after nightfall the next day. Exceptions to this rule are sick people and pregnant women.

Washing   According to Halachah, washing for pleasure is forbidden on Yom Kippur. Washing for health purposes, on the other hand, is permitted.

Anointing   Halachah teaches that another way of "afflicting our souls" on Yom Kippur is by leaving off the perfumes and body oils that we might normally wear.

Wearing leather shoes   One explanation for the Halachah forbidding us to wear leather shoes on Yom Kippur is that this is a good time to renew concern not only for other people but also for the animal kingdom.

Halachah makes it clear that people should not spend

Yom Kippur thinking of new ways to torture themselves. Instead, they should refrain from certain normal activities and concentrate on self-improvement.

REVIEW IT

1. According to Halachah, what are four ways of observing the commandment to afflict our souls on Yom Kippur? What do all four observances have in common?

2. How does Halachah unite Jews of different backgrounds?

Halachah is not in heaven

According to the Aggadah, Moses once begged God, "Please show me the final truth in every matter of Halachah." God said to Moses, "There is no such thing as final truth in Halachah. Every generation has its own truth, which is determined by the majority opinion of its scholars." The following story shows the power of the majority in deciding Halachah. Look for an answer to this question as you read:

What is the advantage of having people decide Halachah democratically?

HUMAN MINDS INTERPRET THE TORAH

One day, the rabbis were arguing about a point of Halachah. Rabbi Eliezer used every argument in trying to win the others over to his point of view. But the other rabbis continued to disagree with him.

Rabbi Eliezer called on the forces of nature to support his arguments. "If I am right, may this carob tree move a hundred yards from its place." The tree moved. But the other rabbis insisted, "No proof can be brought from a carob tree."

Rabbi Eliezer decided to try again. "If I am right about this Halachah, let the stream of water that runs outside our academy flow backward." The stream reversed its course.

Even though the academy walls sagged to signal their agreement with Rabbi Eliezer, Rabbi Joshua would not give in.

But the other rabbis were not impressed. "No proof can be brought from a stream of water."

Unwilling to yield, Rabbi Eliezer tried a third time. "If the Halachah agrees with me, let the walls of the academy prove it." The walls of the academy began to cave in.

Rabbi Joshua spoke harshly to the walls: "If scholars have a disagreement about the Halachah, how does that concern you?"

Out of respect for Rabbi Joshua the walls did not cave in completely, but out of respect for Rabbi Eliezer they did not quite straighten up. Both rabbis were very important, and yet each had a different approach to Halachah.

This time Rabbi Eliezer called on heaven directly to settle the question.

"If I am right about the Halachah, let heaven prove it," he said.

In response to Rabbi Eliezer's call, a heavenly echo said to the other rabbis, "Why are you arguing with Rabbi Eliezer? His opinion about matters of Halachah is correct."

You might think this would have ended the argument. But another rabbi rose and said, "There is no reason for us to pay any attention to a voice from heaven. The Torah is not in heaven. It was given to us from Mount Sinai. And the Torah itself tells us, 'You are to decide by a majority.' Rabbi Eliezer is clearly in the minority."

Later, one of the rabbis met the prophet Elijah and asked him, "What did God do when He heard how we refused to listen to the heavenly echo?"

Elijah answered, "God laughed with joy and said, 'My children have defeated Me.'"

This Aggadah teaches that God is pleased when people who know Torah refuse to base Halachah on miracles but insist on deciding Halachah democratically.

REVIEW IT

1. Why did the other rabbis not accept Rabbi Eliezer's point of view even though the heavenly echo agreed with him?

2. What did God mean when He said, "My children have defeated Me"?

SEE FOR YOURSELF

The great debate on Halachah in which the democratic spirit of the rabbis "defeated" God is told in the Talmud at Baba Metzia 59a–b.

The commandment to "afflict your souls" on Yom Kippur is given in the Torah at Leviticus 23:27. The exact wording in English will depend on which edition you choose: one recent translation reads "you shall practice self-denial."

הַפְטָרָה

HAFTARAH
häf·tä·rä'

The **Haftarah** is the passage from one of the books of the Prophets—Nevi'im—that follows the Torah reading on Shabbat and holidays. Although Haftarah is sometimes pronounced with an o sound, as häf·tōr'ə, it is not related to the word "Torah." Haftarah means "conclusion": it comes at the conclusion of the Torah ceremony and is usually related in some way to the ideas in the Torah portion.

At a Bar or Bat Mitzvah, as at every traditional Torah service, the Haftarah follows the Torah reading.

CHAPTER THREE

The picture shows the prophet Isaiah addressing the Jews in exile in Babylonia. He is describing the connection he sees between the exile and the flood that covered the earth in the time of Noah. At first glance, each event seemed terribly destructive. Yet by wiping out an evil world, the flood enabled humanity to begin again with a clean slate. In the same way, says Isaiah, the exile created a great deal of suffering, but the experience will have a positive effect in the end. After the flood, God promised Noah that He would never again bring another flood to destroy the earth. In the same way, following the exile, God now promises that He will live with His people in kindness and peace.

For many centuries, Jews have followed the Torah reading of the story of Noah and the flood with the Haftarah that contains Isaiah's comforting words.

In this chapter, you will learn that the meaning of the Haftarah is often related in some way either to the Torah portion or to the holiday on which the Haftarah is read. In the second section you will learn two stories that show how Jewish practices may begin.

CHAPTER SUMMARY

Lesson 1: The Haftarah sometimes gives a broader meaning to an incident mentioned in the Torah reading.

Lesson 2: The practice of reading the Haftarah may have started in response to the needs of a particular time in Jewish history.

The Book of Jonah as Haftarah

On Yom Kippur afternoon, we read the entire Book of Jonah as the Haftarah. If you remember the story of Jonah, what may stick in your mind is the fish that swallowed him. But after you finish reading this section, you should be able to answer this question:

How does the Haftarah we read on Yom Kippur afternoon affect the Torah reading for that service?

HAVE YOU HEARD?

The Book of Isaiah reflects the ideas of at least two Prophets. "First Isaiah" lived about 2700 years ago, during the time when Assyria conquered the Northern Kingdom (Israel). "Second Isaiah," who preached to the Jews in exile in Babylonia, lived about two centuries later.

◁ Isaiah's message of comfort to the Jews of Babylon is recorded in the Haftarah that we read after the story of Noah in the Torah portion.

THE BOOK OF JONAH TEACHES ABOUT GOD'S FORGIVENESS

In the afternoon Torah portion for Yom Kippur, we read that God instructed Moses to tell the Hebrews not to follow the ways of the people of Egypt or of Canaan. According to the Torah reading, if any Hebrews followed these ways, they would die.

For the Haftarah we read the Book of Jonah. This book tells of a Jewish Prophet, Jonah, whom God sent to the non-Jewish kingdom of Nineveh. The Ninevites' immoral and violent ways of dealing with one another displeased God. Jonah was to warn them that God would destroy them for their sins. (Although the idea that God punishes people directly may no longer seem real to us, this was the way that ancient people understood life's hardships.)

At first Jonah did not do his task. He wanted to escape the job because he did not think that urging these non-Jews to repent was worth the trouble. So Jonah ran away. He boarded a ship to take him far from home. By running away, he hoped to avoid a second command from God to deliver the message.

But Jonah's plan did not work. God threatened the ship with a terrible storm. Jonah finally admitted to the ship's crew that his fleeing from God had caused the storm. He told the sailors to toss him overboard to save the ship. The sailors did not want to harm Jonah in any way. Only when they failed to bring the ship to shore did they reluctantly toss Jonah overboard. Immediately the sea calmed down.

Then a great fish swallowed Jonah. After living in the fish's belly for three days, Jonah prayed to God. The fish then threw Jonah up on dry land.

When God asked Jonah a second time to go to the Ninevites, Jonah obeyed. When they heard about God's anger, the people of Nineveh did repent. And much to Jonah's annoyance, God decided not to punish them.

This time God used a vine to teach Jonah a lesson. At first God grew a vine over Jonah's head to protect him from the sun. The next day God made the vine wither. Jonah was very angry.

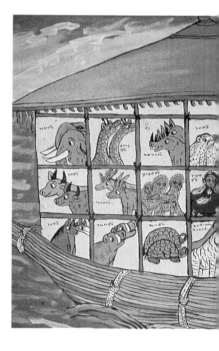

HAVE YOU HEARD?

The kingdom of Nineveh (nin'ə • və) was located on the Tigris River, in what is now northern Iraq. At one time, Nineveh held many thousands of people, called Ninevites (nin'ə • vīts). Nineveh was the capital of the powerful Assyrian Empire during the seventh century B.C.E. Babylonian invaders destroyed Nineveh in 612 B.C.E., only 26 years before the Babylonians captured Jerusalem and destroyed the First Temple.

An Ethiopian scroll painting of Noah's ark.

God said to him, "If you feel so sorry the vine was destroyed, how do you think I would feel about the death of more than 120,000 Ninevites who can't tell right from wrong?"

On Yom Kippur we ask God to forgive us for whatever bad things we may have done during the year. The Torah portion in the afternoon describes the behavior of some non-Jewish ancient peoples that God found unacceptable. The Haftarah teaches that if people repent—are really sorry for having done wrong—and seek God's forgiveness, God will forgive them. God forgives all people, not only Jews, if they truly repent. Jews should not begrudge other people God's love and forgiveness.

REVIEW IT

1. The Torah portion on Yom Kippur afternoon tells Jews of their special relationship with God. Whose practices should they avoid?

2. Which two lessons does the Haftarah from the Book of Jonah add to the Torah reading? (a) God will punish all Jews who follow the ways of other nations. (b) God will forgive Jews but not non-Jews if they repent. (c) God will forgive anyone who truly repents. (d) Jews should be willing to share God's love and forgiveness with other people.

3. Have you ever learned a lesson indirectly, as did Jonah in the incident with the vine?

WHAT TIME IS IT?

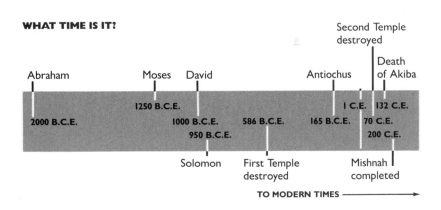

How the practice of reading the Haftarah began

We know that the practice of reading the Haftarah goes back to ancient times. No one knows for sure how it began, but there are two interesting possibilities. As you read about both possibilities, look for answers to these questions:

a. How do the blessings chanted before and after the Haftarah help remind us of the importance of the Prophets' messages?
b. How does the idea of Haftarah show how Judaism is always growing?

THE SAMARITANS AND THE HAFTARAH

For nearly 28 centuries, a community of people called Samaritans has lived in Samaria, on the West Bank of the Jordan River. Although the Samaritans are not Jews, they strictly observe the laws in the Torah. They do not, however, believe that the Hebrew Prophets spoke the word of God.

The Jewish leaders of long ago worried that the people might be influenced by the Samaritan belief that only the Torah is the word of God. These leaders may have started the practice of the Haftarah to show the holiness of the words of the Prophets along with the Torah. The Jews would hear a portion from the Prophets read each week after the Torah portion. This practice would show that both portions were God's word.

The blessings we chant before and after the Haftarah suggest that this "Samaritan theory" of the origin of the Haftarah may be correct. The blessing before the reading stresses that the words of the Prophets were inspired by God. God chose these Prophets, just as He chose the Torah, Moses, and the people of Israel:

This clay storage jar was made in the land of Israel at least 2600 years ago, between the era of David and Solomon and the time of the exile to Babylonia.

בָּרוּךְ אַתָּה, יְיָ אֱלֹהֵינוּ, מֶלֶךְ הָעוֹלָם, אֲשֶׁר בָּחַר בִּנְבִיאִים טוֹבִים,
וְרָצָה בְדִבְרֵיהֶם הַנֶּאֱמָרִים בֶּאֱמֶת. בָּרוּךְ אַתָּה יְיָ, הַבּוֹחֵר בַּתּוֹרָה,
וּבְמֹשֶׁה עַבְדּוֹ, וּבְיִשְׂרָאֵל עַמּוֹ, וּבִנְבִיאֵי הָאֱמֶת וָצֶדֶק.

After reading the Haftarah, we thank God for honoring us by giving us not only the Torah, Shabbat (or the particular holiday), and the chance to worship Him, but also the Prophets:

עַל הַתּוֹרָה, וְעַל הָעֲבוֹדָה, וְעַל הַנְּבִיאִים, וְעַל יוֹם הַשַּׁבָּת הַזֶּה,
שֶׁנָּתַתָּ לָּנוּ, יְיָ אֱלֹהֵינוּ, לִקְדֻשָּׁה וְלִמְנוּחָה, לְכָבוֹד וּלְתִפְאָרֶת.

By repeating that God gave us both the Torah and the Books of the Prophets, the blessings before and after the Haf-

When you prepare for your Bar or Bat Mitzvah, you too will have your teacher's or rabbi's guidance in learning your Haftarah. The Haftarah shown here is from Isaiah and follows a Torah reading from Leviticus.

tarah may have originally reminded the people of the difference between Samaritan and Jewish beliefs.

ANTIOCHUS AND THE HAFTARAH

According to another story, the practice of reading the Haftarah may have begun during the time of the Syrian King Antiochus. Antiochus wanted all his subjects to worship the Greek gods. On Ḥanukkah we recall how he mistreated his Jewish subjects. He forbade them to read or study the Torah.

But the Jews found a way to get around this cruel law. Instead of reading the forbidden Torah portion of the week, they read a selection from the Prophets that reminded them in some way of the Torah portion.

By the time the Jews had defeated Antiochus, they had become used to reading the Haftarah. This practice has continued through the ages to our own time.

REVIEW IT

1. In what important ways do the Samaritan and Antiochus stories differ as possible explanations for the origin of the Haftarah?

2. Discuss one personal custom you have followed for so long you can't remember when you started.

HAVE YOU HEARD?

The Syrian King Antiochus (an • tī′ ə • kəs) gave himself the title Epiphanes (ə• pif′ ə • nēz), which is Greek for "the visible god." He behaved with such insane cruelty that his subjects instead gave him the name Epimanes (ə• pim′ ə • nēz), or "the madman."

חוּמָשׁ

ḤUMASH

ḥoo · mäsh'

Ḥumash comes from חָמֵשׁ, the Hebrew word for "five." In English, the Ḥumash is sometimes called the Pentateuch. The Ḥumash is also called the Five Books of Moses.

The Five Books of Moses make up the Ḥumash, which comes from the Hebrew word for "five."

23

The Ḥumash is the first five books of the Bible. Sometimes when people talk about the Torah, they mean the Ḥumash as opposed to the Books of the Prophets (Nevi'im) or the Writings (Ketuvim). In English, each of the five books of the Ḥumash is named after the book's main theme. The Hebrew name comes from one of the book's first significant words. The chart on the next page lists the Hebrew and English titles and summarizes the contents of each book.

The Ḥumash combines history, stories, poems, and laws. This chapter concentrates on some of the stories in the Ḥumash. The first section tells about a famous struggle between brothers. The second section describes how some Biblical heroes met their wives.

CHAPTER SUMMARY

Lesson 1: The stories in the Ḥumash show us that our ancestors had human failings and ambitions just as we do.

Lesson 2: We can learn that our ancestors had distinct personalities by comparing similar stories about them in the Ḥumash.

HAVE YOU HEARD?

In Greek, Pentateuch (pen'tə • to͞ok) means "five books." Another word with Greek roots is "Bible," which comes from a Greek word meaning "book." The same word is the source of the name Byblos, a Mediterranean city (near present-day Beirut) famous in ancient times as an exporter of papyrus.

◁ Thinking that Isaac was about to die, Rebecca dressed Jacob up to be hairy like Esau, so that the old man would give Jacob a blessing.

Learning from the stories in the Ḥumash

Why does the Ḥumash open with the creation of the world and not with the story of Abraham? After all, Jewish history begins with Abraham, who does not even appear until the end of the eleventh chapter! By including the stories of creation and of the generations before Abraham, the Ḥumash teaches that God created the entire universe and that all people, not merely Jews, are His children.

Just as the opening stories of the Ḥumash teach us important lessons, so do all the later stories. As you read, ask yourself:

What do we learn from the stories of Esau's birthright and Isaac's blessing?

The Ḥumash חוּמָשׁ

ENGLISH TITLE	MEANING	HEBREW TITLE	MEANING	CONTENTS
Genesis	From the Greek for "origin"	בְּרֵאשִׁית	In the beginning	Creation of the world, early history of the Hebrews
Exodus	From the Greek for "departure"	שְׁמוֹת	Names (of Jacob's sons who came into Egypt)	Departure from slavery in Egypt, receiving of the Torah
Leviticus	From the Greek for "having to do with the Levites," members of the priestly tribe of Levi	וַיִּקְרָא	And He called	Laws for the priests and rituals
Numbers	From the census that took place in the desert	בְּמִדְבַּר	In the desert	Forty years through the desert, to the borders of the Promised Land
Deuteronomy	From the Greek for "repetition of the law"	דְּבָרִים	Words	Moses repeats God's laws for the people who have grown up in the desert

OUR ANCESTORS HAD HUMAN FAILINGS AND AMBITIONS

After Abraham's son Isaac married Rebecca, they had twin sons. Esau, their hairy older son, loved hunting. Jacob, the smooth-skinned younger twin, preferred to study. Before the twins were born, Rebecca had learned from God that Jacob would become the head of the family. But Isaac preferred his older son, who made good food for him from the animals he killed.

In those days, after a father's death, the oldest son received twice as much of his father's land and possessions as the other sons. This privilege was called the oldest son's birthright. In the twins' case, the birthright also included Abraham's agreement with God. God would bless Abraham's offspring and give them the Promised Land. In return, Abraham's offspring would worship God and spread His teachings.

Esau returned home from the hunt one day to find his brother cooking a thick vegetable soup. Esau demanded some, saying, "I'm so hungry I'll even sell you my birthright for some of that soup." Esau did not think very much of his birthright.

Some time after, Rebecca overheard Isaac say to Esau: "Fetch an animal from the woods, cook it up into a tasty dish, and then I shall bless you before I die."

Rather than allow the blessing of Abraham to pass through Isaac to Esau, Rebecca decided to take matters into her own hands. While Esau was out hunting, she told Jacob to bring her two goats from the flock. She prepared a dish for Isaac from the goats. Then she dressed Jacob in an outfit of Esau's. She used the goatskins to cover Jacob's smooth arms, so they would feel like Esau's hairy arms if Isaac touched him. She knew that Isaac had become blind with old age and would not be able to see which of his sons had brought him the food.

The trick worked. Isaac thought he was blessing Esau when he said, "May you rule over your brothers."

This Hebrew scroll, containing parts of the Ḥumash, was made by Jews in China, probably during the fifteenth century C.E. It was copied from scrolls brought centuries earlier from the land of Israel.

We learn some important lessons from the stories of Esau's birthright and the trick played on Isaac. One is that all people, even our forefather Isaac, have weaknesses. Isaac's love of good food kept him from knowing the truth. Another lesson is that all people can learn from their mistakes. Some time after Isaac learned he had been tricked, he sent Jacob off to marry a good woman from his mother's family. As Jacob left, Isaac gave him the blessing of Abraham, this time knowing he was blessing Jacob and that Jacob was the worthier son. A third lesson is that Jacob the student is a better model for us than Esau the hunter, even though Jacob may have been too eager to receive his father's blessing.

REVIEW IT

1. What might be one reason the Ḥumash begins with eleven chapters about the whole world instead of focusing immediately on the ancient Hebrews?

2. Who was (a) fooled by his love of good food? (b) too eager to have a blessing? (c) not interested enough in having a blessing? (d) willing to cheat for a favorite son?

Comparing similar stories in the Ḥumash

Finding the right person to marry has always been important. In the Ḥumash, we learn that three important figures in our history found their wives in foreign lands beside a well. By comparing the three similar stories, we learn that our ancestors had very distinct personalities. Read on to learn how Isaac, Jacob, and Moses each found a wife, and ask:

How do the different ways Isaac, Jacob, and Moses each found a wife reveal their different personalities?

FINDING A BRIDE BESIDE A WELL

Isaac and Rebecca   Isaac did not actually find his wife, Rebecca, beside a well. His father's servant Eliezer did the finding for him. Abraham charged Eliezer to find a wife for

SEE FOR YOURSELF

The story of Isaac, Esau, and Jacob comes from Genesis 27–28:4. The three meetings at the well are: Isaac and Rebecca, Genesis 24:10–61; Jacob and Rachel, Genesis 29:1–20; and Moses and Zipporah, Exodus 2:15–21.

Rachel's meeting with Jacob is one of three famous "well stories" in the Ḥumash.

Isaac from among Abraham's own family. He did not want Isaac to marry a Canaanite woman who might influence Isaac to worship her people's gods.

Rebecca was the daughter of one of Abraham's kinsmen. But Eliezer did not choose her for Isaac for that reason alone. Before Rebecca arrived at the well, Eliezer spoke to God. He said he would look for this sign in a woman to prove she would be a good wife: he would ask her to draw water only for himself, but on her own she would offer to give water to his camels, too. Rebecca passed Eliezer's test by drawing water first for him and then for his camels. Eliezer then took out many gifts for her family.

Rebecca ran home to inform her family of Eliezer's arrival. Her brother Laban immediately noticed Eliezer's gifts. Laban then invited Eliezer back to their home for a meal. Although Rebecca's family wanted her to stay with them another year before leaving to marry Isaac, she chose to go right away.

Jacob and Rachel Unlike Eliezer, Jacob arrived at the well without any gifts. He was running away from his brother Esau. At the well, he met a group of shepherds. He asked them about his uncle Laban. Soon, Rachel arrived at the well, leading her father Laban's sheep. Jacob first removed by himself the heavy stone that covered the top of the well. Then he drew water for his uncle's flock.

When Jacob told Rachel who he was, she ran home to tell her father. Laban greeted him nicely. But before long, Laban was to cheat Jacob. Jacob loved Rachel so much that he agreed to work seven years for Laban in order to win Rachel as his wife. But after the seven years had passed, Laban substituted his older daughter Leah. Jacob then had to work another seven years before he finally won his beloved Rachel.

Moses and Zipporah Like Jacob, Moses arrived at the well as a fugitive. He had fled to the land of Midian from Egypt, where he had killed an Egyptian who had beaten a Hebrew slave. At the well, Moses met seven daughters of a priest of Midian, leading their father's flock. A group of shepherds chased the girls away. But Moses saved the girls from the shepherds and drew water for them to give the flock.

When the girls told their father how Moses had saved them, he invited Moses home for a meal. He gave Moses not only a job as a shepherd but also his daughter Zipporah as a wife.

REVIEW IT

1. From what you know about Isaac and Rebecca as parents, does it seem significant that Isaac was not even present at the well and that Rebecca was the only woman to draw water herself at the well? What do these facts suggest about the personalities of Isaac and Rebecca?

2. What positive Jewish value did Rebecca show at the well?

3. What hint of Laban's behavior toward Jacob can you find in his behavior with Eliezer?

4. Why is it important to know that Moses saved the girls from the shepherds? Can you think of some other incidents in Moses' life in which water was very important?

כְּתוּבִים

KETUVIM
kə · tōō · vēm′

Ketuvim, or "Writings," is the third part of the Bible. The Hebrew word for Bible, or Tanach (תַּנַ"ךְ), is an abbreviation of its three parts: the ת stands for Torah, the נ stands for Nevi'im (נְבִיאִים), and the ךְ stands for כְּתוּבִים.

The old-fashioned quill pen and inkpot should remind you that "Ketuvim" means "Writings."

CHAPTER FIVE

A s you can see from the chart on page 34, Ketuvim contains many different types of books. The 150 hymns in the Book of Psalms are religious poems representing many different human emotions. The sayings in the Book of Proverbs are meant as guides for everyday life. The Book of Job deals with the suffering of a good and God-fearing man. The five scrolls, or Megillot (מְגִלּוֹת), which we read during the course of the year, are very different from one another. Ketuvim also includes several books that deal with the period before, during, and after the Babylonian exile.

This chapter introduces you to some of the books of Ketuvim. You will learn first about some lessons taught in the Book of Proverbs. Next you will learn the occasion on which each of the Megillot is read.

CHAPTER SUMMARY

Lesson 1: The ideal life described in the Book of Proverbs combines honesty, hard work, and kindness to others.

Lesson 2: Each of the five Megillot is read on a special day of the year.

The Book of Proverbs

You may already be familiar with some sayings from the Book of Proverbs without knowing it. For example, "Spare the rod and spoil the child" comes from the Book of Proverbs. As you read more about this part of the Ketuvim, ask yourself:

a. What does the Book of Proverbs say about the duties parents and children owe each other?
b. What does the Book of Proverbs say about accepting criticism from parents and others?

PARENTS' AND CHILDREN'S DUTIES TO EACH OTHER

According to the Book of Proverbs, parents have the responsibility to show their children the right road to follow. If they do so, the children will continue along that road even in old

◁ Two North African Jews study Ketuvim, which holds wisdom for every age, place, and season.

Ketuvim כְּתוּבִים

ENGLISH TITLE	HEBREW TITLE	CONTENTS
Psalms	תְּהִלִּים	Hymns of praise, attributed to David.
Proverbs	מִשְׁלֵי	Wise sayings, ascribed to Solomon.
Job	אִיּוֹב	The faith of Job, a righteous man, is tested through suffering.

MEGILLOT מְגִלּוֹת		
Song of Songs	שִׁיר הַשִּׁירִים	Poem in praise of love, traditionally ascribed to Solomon.
Ruth	רוּת	Ruth, a Moabite woman, shows her unselfishness and loyalty by befriending her mother-in-law Naomi.
Lamentations	אֵיכָה	A sad song (elegy), traditionally believed to have been written by Jeremiah after the destruction of Jerusalem.
Ecclesiastes	קֹהֶלֶת	Maxims and meditations on the meaning of life, traditionally attributed to Solomon.
Esther	אֶסְתֵּר	The Purim story.

Daniel	דָּנִיֵּאל	Describes Daniel's exile in Babylonia, then claims to reveal the future.
Ezra	עֶזְרָא	History of two leaders who helped the Jews reestablish life in Eretz Yisrael after the return from exile.
Nehemiah	נְחֶמְיָה	
I Chronicles	דִּבְרֵי הַיָּמִים א	Reviews history from the beginning of the world to the end of the Babylonian captivity.
II Chronicles	דִּבְרֵי הַיָּמִים ב	

age. "Start your children on the right road, and they will not leave it even when they grow old."

Correcting a child who has strayed from the path is just as important as showing him the right path to begin with. It is in this connection that we find the proverb, "A father who spares the rod hates his child, but the one who loves him keeps him in order."

Children also have certain responsibilities toward their parents. One proverb compares parents' teachings to jewelry, and advises children to pay attention to those teachings: "Pay attention to what your father and mother teach you, for their teachings are a wreath around your head and a necklace of honor around your neck."

Children should also be careful not to say nasty things to their parents or about them. The Book of Proverbs describes those who speak ill of their parents: "Their teeth are swords, their jaws are knives, ready to devour the poor."

ACCEPTING ADVICE FROM PARENTS AND OTHERS

The Book of Proverbs teaches that we should be ready to accept criticism from our parents. Only fools ignore their criticism. "A wise man understands why his father is correcting him. A clown ignores criticism."

We should also appreciate criticism from other people. One proverb teaches that whoever loves knowledge loves to be corrected. Another teaches that only a fool thinks he is always right. A third proverb suggests that we are better off being wounded by a friend than kissed by an enemy. In other words, criticism from someone who cares about you is more valuable than flattery from someone who doesn't.

The Book of Proverbs also teaches that allowing our ideas to be criticized can help us think them through. "Just as iron sharpens iron, so one person can sharpen the ideas of another."

So the next time someone argues with something you have said, don't take offense. Perhaps you can benefit from the criticism. "To despise a word of advice is to bring trouble on yourself."

An Israeli artist based this tapestry on the Book of Ruth, one of the books of Ketuvim. The tapestry illustrates the book's last line, which shows that Ruth and Boaz were the ancestors of King David.

REVIEW IT

1. What does the idea of sharpening one iron object by rubbing it against another have to do with accepting criticism from others?

2. Create some proverbs of your own about (a) loyalty to friends, (b) fairness in school or play, (c) accepting criticism.

The five Megillot

What does the word Megillah (מְגִלָה) make you think of? Maybe you know the expression "the whole Megillah," which means "the whole story." Probably the word makes you think of the story of Queen Esther that we read from a scroll in synagogue on Purim. In fact, Megillah means "scroll." There are four other Megillot besides the scroll of Esther. All five Megillot are in the Ketuvim section of the Tanach. Each Megillah is read from a scroll on a special day of the Jewish calendar. As you read, ask yourself:

What are the five Megillot and when are they read?

READING THE MEGILLOT

The first of the Megillot is called the Song of Songs, or שִׁיר הַשִׁירִים. The Song of Songs is read on Pesaḥ, which is sometimes called the springtime holiday. Some of the most beautiful love poems in any language come from the Song of Songs, which tells of two lovers in springtime. The rabbis of the Talmud decided that the Song of Songs really tells about God's love for the Children of Israel. God freed the Hebrews from slavery in the spring.

On Shavuot, we recall God's gift of the Torah. Shavuot is also the holiday when the first fruits of the land were given to God in the Temple in Jerusalem. On this holiday, we read the second Megillah, the Book of Ruth (רוּת), for two reasons. First, the story of Ruth takes place during the springtime

These pictures should help you remember the five Megillot. From lower left to upper right: for the Song of Songs, music and young love; for the Book of Ruth, the spring harvest; for the Book of Lamentations, the Temple in flames; for Ecclesiastes, a sukkah, because Megillat Kohelet is read on Sukkot; and for the Book of Esther, familiar parts of the Purim festival.

HAVE YOU HEARD?

The First Temple was built by King Solomon around 950 B.C.E. Construction of the Second Temple took place between 520 and 515 B.C.E., after the first wave of exiles had returned from Babylonia to Jerusalem. It was this Second Temple that Judah Maccabee recaptured and cleansed in 165 B.C.E. Rebuilt about 150 years later, the Second Temple was destroyed by Roman legions on the ninth day of the month of Av in the year 70 C.E.

רוּת

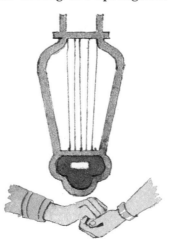

שִׁיר הַשִׁירִים

קֹהֶלֶת

אֶסְתֵּר

אֵיכָה

harvest. Second, Ruth, the non-Jewish daughter-in-law of Naomi, accepted the laws of the Torah.

The third Megillah, the Book of Lamentations, does not contain a happy story. We read this Megillah, called אֵיכָה, on Tisha b'Av. This special day, the ninth day of the month of Av, comes during the summer. On it, we remember the destruction of both the First and the Second Temples in Jerusalem. The First Temple was destroyed by the King of Babylon in 586 B.C.E. Many Jews were killed, and many were forced to go to Babylon as captives. Megillat אֵיכָה contains sad poems about the fallen Jewish state. But it ends with the prayer to God that we recite each Shabbat and festival when returning the Sefer Torah to the ark: "Turn us to You, O God, and let us return. Let our days be once again like the old days."

הֲשִׁיבֵנוּ יְיָ אֵלֶיךָ, וְנָשׁוּבָה.
חַדֵּשׁ יָמֵינוּ כְּקֶדֶם.

The fourth Megillah is read on Sukkot, the autumn harvest holiday. This Megillah is called Ecclesiastes or קֹהֶלֶת, which means a person who speaks in an assembly. Much of Megillat Kohelet presents a serious view of human existence. This Megillah teaches that there is no purpose in life except to fear God and fulfill His commandments. King Solomon is said to have written Song of Songs in the springtime of his

life, when he was young, and Ecclesiastes in the autumn of his life, when he was growing old.

The fifth Megillah is the Book of Esther. Since the Book of Esther tells the history of the first Purim, you don't really need to be told that we read Megillat Esther at Purim!

Before Sukkot, Jews on New York City's Lower East Side shop carefully for a fragrant etrog and a beautiful lulav branch, festive symbols of the autumn harvest holiday.

REVIEW IT

1. Which two Megillot are gloomier than the other three?

2. How might you explain the fact that more people are familiar with Megillat Esther than with the other Megillot?

לְשׁוֹן הַקֹּדֶשׁ

LESHON HAKODESH
lə · shōn′ hä · kō′desh

Leshon HaKodesh—"the holy language"—is what the rabbis of the Talmud called Hebrew because it is the language in which the Torah was written.

Eliezer ben Yehuda, the father of modern Hebrew.

CHAPTER SIX

The rabbis of old wondered why the Torah begins with the letter bet, the first letter of the Hebrew word בְּרֵאשִׁית, which is the opening word of the first book of the Ḥumash. After all, they felt, the entire alef-bet of Leshon HaKodesh is holy, and even the order of the letters of the alef-bet is holy. So why doesn't the Torah begin with the first letter of the alef-bet, the alef?

One answer they gave shows just how holy they believed Leshon HaKodesh to be. The letter alef is the first letter of the Hebrew word that means "cursed" (אָרוּר). It would have been inappropriate for the Torah to begin with a letter associated with cursing. Instead, the rabbis believed, God said to Himself, "The word for 'blessing' (בְּרָכָה) begins with the letter bet. It is fitting that the holy Torah should begin with the letter of Leshon HaKodesh most closely associated with blessing."

In this chapter you will learn how the alphabet of Leshon HaKodesh helps us remember the Torah's teachings. You will also learn about Eliezer ben Yehuda, whose efforts made Leshon HaKodesh once again a living language.

CHAPTER SUMMARY

Lesson 1: The alphabet of Leshon HaKodesh can help us remember the Torah's teachings.

Lesson 2: The father of modern Hebrew is Eliezer ben Yehuda.

The Hebrew alphabet
helps us study Torah

◁ A page from a thirteenth-century Haggadah shows four of the ten plagues that God brought upon the Egyptians.

When you study for a test, do you ever make up study aids to help you remember some facts? For example, the first letters of the words "**M**y **v**ery **e**xcellent **m**other **j**ust **s**ent **us n**ine **p**izzas" can help you remember the names of the planets in their order from the sun: Mercury, Venus, Earth, Mars, Jupiter, Saturn, Uranus, Neptune, and Pluto. In the same way, the rabbis of the Talmud encourage us to use the alphabet of Leshon HaKodesh to help us remember Torah. Try to answer this question as you read:

What are some ways in which the Hebrew alphabet can help us learn Torah?

NUMBERS AND INITIALS

Each of the 22 letters of the Hebrew alphabet has a number value, as the table opposite the Introduction shows. Every word in Leshon HaKodesh, therefore, also has a number value. To find it, you simply add up the number values of each of the word's letters. We can use the number values to help us remember important teachings of the Torah.

For example, we learn the most important teaching about God in the Torah's statement that we call the Shema. The Shema teaches us that God is One, or, in Leshon Ha-Kodesh, אֶחָד.

If we add the number values of the letters that make up the word אֶחָד, we get $1 + 8 + 4 = 13$. Scholars find this number 13 significant because it reminds them of the passage in the Torah that lists the thirteen kinds of mercy that God shows in His dealings with people. In the Passover Haggadah, the song "Eḥad Mi Yodea"(אֶחָד מִי יוֹדֵעַ, or "Who Knows One?") begins with God as One and ends with God's thirteen qualities of mercy.

The Passover Haggadah also gives an example of another type of alphabetic study aid. Shortly before we sing "Dayenu," we list the ten plagues that God brought upon the Egyptians. As we say the name of each plague, we spill a drop of wine onto a plate. Then we recite three words made up by Rabbi Yehudah, who used the initials of the plagues as a study aid: דְּצַ"ךְ עֲדַ"שׁ בְּאַחַ"ב.

Why did Rabbi Yehudah divide the plagues up into precisely these three groups? The first three plagues, דָּם, צְפַרְדֵּעַ, כִּנִּים—blood, frogs, and lice—Aaron brought about with the use of his staff. The second group of three, עָרֹב, דֶּבֶר, שְׁחִין—flies, cattle disease, boils—Moses brought

SEE FOR YOURSELF

You can find the rabbis' explanation of why the Torah begins with the letter bet in Genesis Rabbah 1:10. The passage in the Torah listing God's thirteen kinds of mercy is Exodus 34:6–7.

On a Tel Aviv street, modern Hebrew mingles with modern English. The man who made Leshon HaKodesh a language suitable for everyday life in Israel was Eliezer ben Yehuda.

about without use of his staff. The final group of four plagues, בָּרָד, אַרְבֶּה, חֹשֶׁךְ, מַכַּת בְּכוֹרוֹת —hail, locusts, darkness, death of the firstborn—Moses brought about by using his staff. So Rabbi Yehudah's study aid helps us remember not only the names of the plagues and their order, but also a difference among the three groups.

Rashi, a famous interpreter of the Ḥumash, suggested that we should all make up our own study aids to help us remember the vast amount of wisdom the Torah contains. Now that you know two types of study aids, you can use the alphabet of Leshon HaKodesh to help you remember Torah.

REVIEW IT

1. The rabbis thought it was significant that the Hebrew words for wine (יַיִן) and secret (סוֹד) added up to the same number. What is that number? Can you think of any reason why the rabbis thought this was so revealing?

2. Sometimes codes are written in English by giving each letter of the alphabet its number value. Write a sentence in English number code, and see if a friend can decode it.

Turning Leshon HaKodesh into a spoken language

In Hebrew school you probably learn Hebrew in at least two ways—through the study of prayers written many years ago and through the study of conversational Hebrew as it is spoken in Israel today. So the notion that Hebrew as Leshon HaKodesh should *not* be used in everyday conversation may seem quite odd to you. But from the time the Jews were exiled until very recently, some Jews felt quite strongly that Leshon HaKodesh was so holy that it should not be used in everyday speech. One man is credited with changing that. As you read about the achievement of Eliezer ben Yehuda, ask yourself:

How did Eliezer ben Yehuda transform Hebrew into a spoken language?

ELIEZER BEN YEHUDA: THE FATHER OF MODERN HEBREW

Eliezer ben Yehuda was born in Eastern Europe in 1858. Political events in Europe led him to believe that the Jews, like all other peoples, should have their own land and their own language. So at the age of 23 he left Europe for Eretz Yisrael.

Upon arriving in Eretz Yisrael, Ben Yehuda told his wife that they would speak only Hebrew together. Their son became the first modern child to grow up speaking Hebrew at home.

Ben Yehuda knew that in order to transform Leshon HaKodesh into a spoken language, many new words would have to be created. After all, ancient Hebrew had no words for the many new discoveries in science or the new developments in politics and literature that had taken place during the last several centuries. So Ben Yehuda began to create new words to meet the demands of modern times.

While bringing the language up-to-date, Ben Yehuda also began work on his *Complete Dictionary of Ancient and Modern Hebrew*. Several volumes of this major work were published before his death in 1922. His widow continued the project until her own death in 1951. The seventeenth and last volume of Ben Yehuda's dictionary was published in 1959.

Ben Yehuda did not live long enough to witness the creation of the State of Israel with Hebrew as its official language. But the State of Israel remembers his efforts. A main street in each of Israel's major cities bears his name.

REVIEW IT

1. Why did Ben Yehuda have to create many new words in Hebrew?

2. Some Jews vigorously opposed Ben Yehuda's efforts. Try to imagine some of their reasons. Then suggest some ways in which Ben Yehuda might have argued with them.

מִדְרָשׁ

MIDRASH

mid · räsh'

Midrash is a type of Jewish literature devoted to Bible interpretation. The interpretations began almost 2500 years ago, when many Jews returned to Israel from exile in Babylonia.

"Midrash" comes from the Hebrew word דָּרַשׁ, meaning "to investigate" or "to search." Searching for new meanings in the Torah can be very exciting, as long as you are true to some of the rules of interpretation.

On seder nights we read the Passover story, which has many Midrashim.

45

The statue you see is an idol carved many, many centuries ago. Abraham's father, Terah, made and sold idols like this. The story about Abraham and the idols in his father's shop does not appear in the Humash. We find it instead in the Midrash. So, many people already know some Midrash.

From time to time, when Terah had errands to do, he left Abraham to mind his shop. One day, a man came in to buy an idol. Abraham said to the man, "How can a grown-up man like you, a man who has lived for many years, worship an idol that I saw my father finish only this morning?" The man left without buying an idol.

Another time when Abraham was minding the shop, a woman brought in a plate of flour. She asked Abraham to offer the flour to the idols. As soon as she left, Abraham took a stick and smashed all the idols but the largest. He then placed the stick in the hand of the large idol.

Soon after, Terah returned from his errands. "What has become of the idols?" asked Terah angrily.

Abraham said, "A woman brought in a plate of flour and asked me to offer it to them. Then a fight broke out among the idols, each of whom wanted to eat before the others. This largest idol picked up the stick you see in its hands and smashed all the others so it could eat all the flour."

Terah spoke very angrily to his son: "How can you expect me to believe your story? I myself made these idols, and I know they can neither speak nor understand."

Quietly, Abraham spoke up: "Then, father, why do you bow down to them? There is but one God to Whom we should pray."

This Midrash is based on the Biblical idea that before Abraham, people didn't believe in one God but instead worshiped idols.

In this chapter, you will become familiar with other Midrashim. In the first section, you will learn that the Passover Haggadah contains many Midrashim. In the second section, you will see an example of how the Midrash interprets a passage from the Humash to teach us a moral lesson.

◁ Abraham's father made idols like this one, which comes from ancient Sumer, the land of Abraham's birth.

47

CHAPTER SUMMARY

Lesson 1: Some Midrashim search for the full meaning of the Bible's laws, while others search for lessons in the Bible's stories.

Lesson 2: Many Midrashim are concerned with teaching the spirit of Jewish tradition more than the laws.

The Passover Haggadah: an old, familiar Midrash

During the Passover seder we read the Passover Haggadah (הַגָּדָה). As we do so, we have a chance to act the parts of rabbis whose careful studies of the Torah produced the Midrash. For the Haggadah records the different interpretations of many scholars, and the delight many took in offering interpretations. After you finish reading this section, you should be able to answer this question:

How do the Midrashim in the Haggadah clarify laws as well as teach lessons about the good things to do in life?

"THIS IS ON ACCOUNT OF WHAT THE LORD DID FOR ME"

When you read a sentence in this or another book, how closely do you pay attention to it? Once you get its meaning, and see how it leads from the sentence before it to the sentence after it, you probably just go right on reading. But, of course, the books of the Bible are not just any books. So, for the rabbis, every sentence in every holy book had to be very carefully considered from every possible angle.

In the Book of Exodus, on the very day of the departure from Egypt, God instructed Moses in the laws of Passover. When Jews celebrate Passover in years to come, matzah must be eaten instead of hametz. The Book of Exodus also says, "You shall tell your son on that day, 'This is on account of what the Lord did for me when I came out of Egypt.' " The

The four sons as they appear in an eighteenth-century Dutch Haggadah.

Midrashim we find collected in the Passover Haggadah teach us several things about this sentence.

A picture of four sons appears in many הַגָּדוֹת (the plural of הַגָּדָה). Why? The Torah uses the word "son" not just in this sentence but in three other sentences to stress how important it is to tell each generation about the Exodus from Egypt.

In the Midrash, the rabbis interpret these four sentences to stand for four different kinds of children. The child the Torah describes in the sentence we are considering is one who is not able to ask a question on his own. The child's parent is therefore required to open up the subject of the Exodus for him.

A second Midrash approaches the sentence from another point of view. The sentence says that the child should be told about the Exodus "on that *day*," meaning the anniversary of the Exodus. Doesn't that word suggest that the story of Exodus should be told during the *daytime*? If so, why do parents tell their children the story at *night*, during the seder?

But the Torah also says, "*This* is on account of what the Lord did for me." According to the Midrash, the word "this" refers to the matzah and maror on the seder table on Passover night. So the rabbis decided that the story should be told on the night of the seder after all.

A third Midrash stresses a different word in our sentence, the word "me." No matter how many centuries after the Exodus you may have been born, you—and every other Jew—must consider yourself as having been set free by God from Egypt. This is a basic part of our common Jewish identity. We were once slaves but have become a free people because of God's deeds on our behalf.

So from a single sentence, the Midrash teaches many different things. One Midrash explores this sentence and tells us what kind of child the parent is addressing. Another Midrash uses the sentence to explain to us why the Passover story is told to the children at night, during the seder. A third Midrash teaches us a basic lesson about our Jewish identity.

REVIEW IT

1. Give one example of a single sentence in the Bible in which the Midrash finds many meanings.

2. If as Jews we think of ourselves as freed slaves, how are we likely to treat other oppressed people?

Moral lessons in the Midrash

The rabbi of your congregation may sometimes draw on the Torah portion of the week to make a moral point in the Shabbat sermon. Your rabbi may also connect an incident in the Torah with a more current event. In doing these things, your rabbi is following in the footsteps of the scholars whose close study of the Tanach led to the Midrash. After you read the section below, you should be able to answer this question:

How does the Midrash use the Bible to show that Moses was a hospitable person?

ENTERTAINING JETHRO

After Moses led the Children of Israel out of Egypt, his father-in-law Jethro came to Moses in the desert. Jethro was a priest of Midian, not a Jew. But when Jethro heard from Moses about God's great deeds in freeing the Israelites from slavery, Jethro said, "Now I know that the Lord is the greatest of all gods." Jethro then made a sacrifice to God, and shared a meal with Moses' brother Aaron and all the elders of Israel.

In studying this section of the Torah, the rabbis wondered, "Why does the Torah not say that Moses shared this meal with them as well?" According to the Midrash, Moses is not mentioned because he did not eat the meal. Instead, he was waiting on Jethro and the others. In doing so, he was following the example set by Abraham, who served the three strangers who came to his home.

HAVE YOU HEARD?

The word "hospitable" (hos′pi • tə • bəl) comes from a Latin word meaning "to receive as a guest." Another word from the same root is "hospitality" (hos • pi • tal′i • tē), which is the Mitzvah of treating guests or strangers in a friendly way. From the same root also comes the word "hospital," reflecting the fact that the first hospitals were refuges for the needy and homeless as well as the sick.

SEE FOR YOURSELF

The story of Abraham, Terah, and the idols is told in Genesis Rabbah 38:13. God's instruction to "tell your son on that day, 'This is on account of what the Lord did for me when I came out of Egypt'" appears at Exodus 13:8. Abraham's hospitality to the three angels is described in Genesis 18:1–8.

A Midrash on hospitality points to the kindness Abraham showed the three strangers who paid him a visit.

The Midrash continues its lesson on the Mitzvah of hospitality by telling a story from the rabbis' own time. Rabban Gamaliel, who was head of the Sanhedrin (the highest Jewish court), once gave a banquet. He invited the other great rabbis who studied with him. The rabbis were happy to accept his invitation. But some of the rabbis felt awkward when they discovered that Rabban Gamaliel intended to wait on them himself. Finally, one of the learned guests, Rabbi Joshua, was able to put their minds at rest.

"It is quite proper for our host to serve us himself even though he is a great scholar," said Rabbi Joshua. "After all, a much greater man even than Rabban Gamaliel personally waited on three strangers who came to his home. I refer, of course, to our forefather Abraham, who entertained the three angels who came to his home."

Staff, students, and guests gather in the beautifully decorated Sukkah of New York's Jewish Theological Seminary. Welcoming guests is part of the spirit of Sukkot.

REVIEW IT

1. According to the Midrash, what Mitzvah was Moses observing in not eating the meal with Jethro?

2. This Midrash strengthens its point by telling a story from the period of the Midrash. Which rabbi is the hero of that story?

3. Can you see connections between two events in your life that at first glance seem unrelated?

מְזוּזָה

MEZUZAH

mə · z͞oo · zä′

Mezuzah is a small case containing a piece of parchment that Jews attach to the doorposts of their homes. On the parchment, the first two paragraphs of the Shema are written.

"Mezuzah" is actually the Hebrew word for doorpost.

Every Mezuzah contains the Shema.

CHAPTER EIGHT

All Mezuzot are alike in certain ways. No matter what the style of the case, every Mezuzah contains a piece of parchment. On the parchment a scribe has written by hand twenty-two lines of Hebrew, consisting of the Shema and two passages from the Ḥumash. These passages instruct us to love God, to teach His commandments, and to post God's words on our doorposts.

In ancient times, people believed that God would protect homes that were marked with a Mezuzah. Today, the Mezuzah is an important way of letting everyone know that the people who live in the house are loyal Jews.

In this chapter, you will learn some stories that show how important Jews have considered the Mezuzah over the centuries. You will also learn why Jews through the ages have considered a Mezuzah to be so valuable even if it is made of inexpensive materials.

CHAPTER SUMMARY

Lesson 1: Many wonderful stories are told about Mezuzot.

Lesson 2: The true value of the Mezuzah is in the idea behind the words it contains.

Why "Shaddai" or shin appears on every Mezuzah

◁ The Mezuzot you see here are very different, but they are all alike in two very important ways. Each of them has the word "Shaddai" or the letter shin, and each holds a piece of parchment bearing twenty-two lines of Torah, including the Shema. A piece of parchment from inside a Mezuzah appears at upper left.

Mezuzot are designed in different ways. Some have an opening through which you can see the word שַׁדַּי, which is written on the back of the parchment within. Other Mezuzot have the word שַׁדַּי displayed on the front. Still other Mezuzot have the letter shin on the front. Read on to learn what the word "Shaddai" and the letter shin stand for, and ask yourself:

What do stories from different times in Jewish history show about the Jews' regard for the Mezuzah?

WONDERFUL STORIES ABOUT MEZUZOT

"Shaddai" is usually translated as "Almighty." The Hebrew letters that make up the word are also the initials of the Hebrew words שׁוֹמֵר דַּלְתוֹת יִשְׂרָאֵל. These words mean "guardian of the doors of Israel." Every Mezuzah bears the word "Shaddai" or its first letter, shin.

Today we place Mezuzot on our doors to let everyone know that we are Jewish. But many Jews in the past believed the Mezuzah actually protected them from harm. Many wonderful stories have come down to us about the protective "power" of Mezuzot.

One story takes place only about two hundred years ago in Austria. The government at the time passed a law calling for the expulsion of all Jews who did not have a job. Many elderly Jews did not have jobs of their own but were supported by their families. In order to prevent the government from expelling these Jews from their homes, the Jewish community invented the job of Mezuzah-installer. The government didn't know how easy it actually was to install one. All it takes is to say two blessings and fasten the Mezuzah to the doorpost!

Another story about Mezuzot is told of a Jew in the ancient Roman Empire, Onkelos ben Kalonimos. The Roman Emperor had forbidden the study of Torah. Onkelos ben Kalonimos was a loyal convert to Judaism who, in fact, translated the Torah into Aramaic, the language of the time. Because Onkelos refused to obey the Emperor's law, the Emperor sent a troop of soldiers to arrest him.

Onkelos greeted the soldiers by quoting passages of the Torah. Instead of arresting him, the soldiers themselves converted to Judaism.

The Emperor sent a second group of soldiers to arrest Onkelos. Once again, Onkelos quoted passages from the Torah. And once again, the soldiers who had come to arrest Onkelos became converts to Judaism.

When the Emperor sent a third group of soldiers to arrest Onkelos, he ordered them not to speak to Onkelos at all. The soldiers seized Onkelos and took him along with them.

On their way to the prison, they passed a Jewish home.

HAVE YOU HEARD?

Sometimes the very same word is pronounced differently in English and Hebrew. For example, the word "Mezuzah" is pronounced mə‧zōōz'ə in English but mə‧zōō‧zä' in Hebrew. Similarly, "Megillah" in English is mə‧gil'ə, in Hebrew mə‧gē‧lä'. The guide given at the beginning of each chapter in this book always shows the correct Hebrew pronunciation.

SEE FOR YOURSELF

The two Torah passages inscribed on parchment inside every Mezuzah are Deuteronomy 6:4–9 and 11:13–21. You can read the original story of Onkelos ben Kalonimos in the Talmud at Avodah Zarah 11a.

Onkelos dazzled the Roman soldiers by telling them about the wondrous power of the Mezuzah.

Onkelos noticed the Mezuzah on the doorpost and decided to dazzle the soldiers with a story.

"This is a Mezuzah," said Onkelos. "The Mezuzah shows how limited the power of a mere king like the Emperor is. A king may live in a palace, but he feels safe only when he has servants standing outside the palace to guard him. By contrast, every Jew living in an ordinary home feels secure. The Mezuzah on a Jewish home is a symbol that God, the Heavenly King, guards the people living inside."

The soldiers were so impressed by Onkelos' description of the Mezuzah, and of God's concern for the Jewish people, that they too became converts to Judaism.

Afraid that his whole army would become Jewish, the Emperor sent no more soldiers after Onkelos ben Kalonimos.

REVIEW IT

1. What words do the letters שדי stand for in addition to being a word for God?

2. How did the story of Onkelos and the history behind the "job" of Mezuzah-installer show people that God is the guardian of the doors of Israel?

3. Why do you think Jews today place Mezuzot on their doors?

The value of a Mezuzah

Jews traditionally carry out Mitzvot with enthusiasm. For this reason, we adorn each Sefer Torah with ornaments, light Shabbat and holiday candles in beautiful candlesticks, and cover our loaves of ḥallah with decorated cloths. For the same reason, even though the important part of the Mezuzah is the parchment inside, we decorate the containers in which we place the parchment. But no matter how plain a Mezuzah is, it is still valuable. It is a constant reminder of our relationship with God. As you read about the value of a Mezuzah, ask yourself:

Why did Rabbi Yehudah HaNasi feel that an inexpensive Mezuzah was more valuable than an expensive gem?

RABBI YEHUDAH HANASI AND THE MEZUZAH

As you know, many rabbis are spoken of and quoted in the Talmud. But whenever the Talmud refers to "Rabbi" without giving the rabbi's name, it means the great scholar Rabbi Yehudah. Rabbi Yehudah was called "HaNasi"—the Prince.

Rabbi Yehudah HaNasi is best known for having edited the first part of the Talmud, the Mishnah. He is also known for his wealth, which he used to support many famous scholars.

Besides being honored by the Jewish community, Rabbi

HAVE YOU HEARD?

The Mezuzah should be attached on the right-hand side as you enter; it should be no more than one-third of the way down from the top of the doorpost. Before attaching the Mezuzah, we say two blessings. The first declares that God has commanded us to fasten the Mezuzah:

בָּרוּךְ אַתָּה, יְיָ אֱלֹהֵינוּ, מֶלֶךְ הָעוֹלָם, אֲשֶׁר קִדְּשָׁנוּ בְּמִצְוֹתָיו, וְצִוָּנוּ לִקְבֹּעַ מְזוּזָה.

In the second blessing, we thank God for keeping us alive:

בָּרוּךְ אַתָּה, יְיָ אֱלֹהֵינוּ, מֶלֶךְ הָעוֹלָם, שֶׁהֶחֱיָנוּ, וְקִיְּמָנוּ, וְהִגִּיעָנוּ לַזְּמַן הַזֶּה.

All it takes to install a
Mezuzah is to say two
blessings and fasten the
Mezuzah to the doorpost.

Yehudah was a friend of many Roman officials and of many other heads of state.

One of Rabbi Yehudah's important non-Jewish friends was King Arteban of Parthia. As a sign of their friendship, King Arteban sent Rabbi Yehudah an expensive gem. The messenger who delivered the gem to Rabbi Yehudah also brought this message from the King: "To show that our friendship means as much to you as to me, please send me in return a token of equal value."

Rabbi Yehudah took the gem from the messenger and listened to the message. The messenger lifted his eyebrows in surprise when Rabbi Yehudah placed in his hands a plain Mezuzah. He said nothing, however, and returned to Parthia.

Some time later, Rabbi Yehudah was again visited by the same Parthian messenger. But this time Arteban's message was one of annoyance, not of friendship: "I sent you a priceless gift. The token you gave me in return is worth only a few pennies at most."

"Your king does not understand the value of a Mezuzah, then," said Rabbi Yehudah. "Please tell King Arteban that the gift he sent me is one that I have to worry about guarding. On the other hand, the Mezuzah I sent him guards anyone who understands its true value. The Mezuzah is much more valuable than even the most costly gem, because the Mezuzah is a reminder of the teachings of God's Torah."

REVIEW IT

1. How did Rabbi Yehudah HaNasi's definition of value differ from King Arteban's definition?

2. Which gift *needed* a guard and which gift *was* a guard in the story of Rabbi Yehudah?

מִנְהָג

MINHAG
min · häg′

A **Minhag** is a Jewish custom. Different Minhagim developed at different times and in different places. As a result, the same Halachah may have many different Minhagim attached to it.

How many candles we light on Shabbat is a matter of Minhag.

CHAPTER NINE

Why do many Jews eat fish as a first course for Shabbat dinner? No Halachah tells us to, but there are many reasons for this Minhag. We read in the Ḥumash that when God created the world, He specifically blessed the creation of the fifth, sixth, and seventh days only. Fish were created on the fifth day, people on the sixth day, and Shabbat on the seventh day. Some say that the Minhag of eating fish on Shabbat arose in order to ensure a triple blessing.

There is another reason for the Minhag of eating fish on Shabbat and holidays. The Torah is often compared to water. Just as fish cannot live long outside of water, so the Jewish people cannot survive without the Torah.

Minhagim (מִנְהָגִים) have been handed down from generation to generation. By the time of the Talmud, many Minhagim were already firmly established. The rabbis of the Talmud and Midrash recognized how important Minhagim are. They taught people to follow the Minhagim of their communities, even though the Minhagim are not Halachah.

In this chapter, you will learn why we observe certain familiar Minhagim. In the first section, you will review the difference between Minhag, Halachah, and Mitzvah. The second section explains some favorite Minhagim for the festival of Ḥanukkah.

CHAPTER SUMMARY

Lesson 1: The number of Shabbat candles we light on Friday nights is a matter of Minhag.

Lesson 2: Although Ḥanukkah is only a minor holiday, we observe it with many Minhagim.

Comparing Minhag to Halachah and Mitzvah

Many Jews observe the Mitzvah of lighting candles on Friday night. But candle lighting is practiced with slightly different Minhagim in different Jewish homes. As you read, see which Minhag is most familiar to you, and ask yourself:

What does Minhag add to the Halachah for candle lighting on Erev Shabbat?

◁ Eating unleavened bread on Passover is a Mitzvah, but Minhag determines what shape that bread takes. Instead of the matzot familiar to most of us, these Persian Jews are eating flat, round cakes at their seder.

HOW MANY CANDLES?

One of the first blessings many Jewish children learn is the blessing over the Shabbat candles: "Blessed are You, O Lord our God, King of the Universe, Who has made us holy through His Mitzvot and commanded us to light the Shabbat candle."

בָּרוּךְ אַתָּה, יְיָ אֱלֹהֵינוּ, מֶלֶךְ הָעוֹלָם,
אֲשֶׁר קִדְּשָׁנוּ בְּמִצְוֹתָיו וְצִוָּנוּ לְהַדְלִיק נֵר שֶׁל שַׁבָּת.

The words בְּמִצְוֹתָיו and וְצִוָּנוּ indicate that candle lighting is a Mitzvah.

Halachah gives certain instructions as to how the Mitzvah should be carried out. For example, according to Halachah, Shabbat candles should never be lit any later than eighteen minutes before sunset. But Halachah does not specify the exact number of candles that must be lit.

The number of candles to be lit is a matter of Minhag. The blessing itself talks about a single candle, but the Minhag in most homes is to light two candles. The reason behind this Minhag is related to the two different versions of the Ten Commandments that appear in the Ḥumash. In the first version, the fourth commandment says "Remember the day of Shabbat to keep it holy." In the second version, the fourth commandment says "Observe the day of Shabbat to keep it holy." By following the Minhag to light two Shabbat candles, Jewish families acknowledge both versions of the fourth commandment.

In other families, the Minhag is different. Some people light seven candles, standing for the seven days of Creation or for the seven branches of the menorah that stood in the Temple in Jerusalem. Other people light ten candles, one for each of the Ten Commandments. In still other homes, a candle is lit for each family member.

So you see, there can be many different Minhagim for observing a single Mitzvah where Halachah has not laid down specific rules.

Playing dreidel is a favorite Minhag for Ḥanukkah.

SEE FOR YOURSELF

You can find the two versions of the fourth commandment at Exodus 20:8 and Deuteronomy 5:12.

REVIEW IT

1. How do you know that candle lighting is a Mitzvah and not a Minhag?

2. What aspect of the Mitzvah of candle lighting is not covered by Halachah?

3. Describe a favorite Minhag that your family follows.

Minhagim for Ḥanukkah

Even though Ḥanukkah is not a Biblical holiday, it is one of the favorite celebrations of Jewish children everywhere. Who wouldn't enjoy a holiday that includes special games and gifts, not to mention delicious foods? But not everyone understands the reasons for the different Minhagim we observe on Ḥanukkah. After reading this section, you should be able to answer this question:

Why do we observe the Ḥanukkah Minhagim of dreidel playing, latke eating, and gift giving?

DREIDELS, LATKES, GIFTS

When the Maccabees defeated the Syrian armies of King Antiochus, the Maccabees found that the Syrians had polluted all the holy oil in the Temple except for a single jar, which they had somehow overlooked. Although there was enough oil to burn only for a single day, the oil miraculously lasted for eight days. The Mitzvah of lighting Ḥanukkah candles for eight nights is related to the miracle of the oil.

The miracle of the oil also explains some Minhagim about Ḥanukkah foods. Pancakes (called latkes in Yiddish and לְבִיבוֹת in Hebrew) are traditional foods that are fried in oil. So are doughnuts, which in Hebrew are called סֻפְגָנִיּוֹת.

The Maccabees set up an independent Jewish state and issued coins in honor of their victory. These coins may explain the Minhag of giving children Ḥanukkah gelt, or money.

The Minhagim we have talked about thus far have their roots in Jewish tradition. But Jews have always lived among other peoples, and some Minhagim are borrowed. Giving gifts at Ḥanukkah is an example of such a Minhag. In the Jewish calendar, Purim is really the traditional time for gift giving. But since Christians exchange gifts at Christmas, Jews have come to exchange gifts other than coins at Ḥanukkah, which comes at the same time of year.

Another Ḥanukkah Minhag for children is the game of dreidel. The dreidel is a four-sided top. On each of the sides appears a Hebrew letter: nun (נ), gimmel (ג), hay (ה), and shin (ש). These letters are the initials of the Hebrew words נֵס גָּדוֹל הָיָה שָׁם —a great miracle happened there. The number value of these four initials equals 358, which happens also to be the number value in Leshon HaKodesh of the word Mashiaḥ, מָשִׁיחַ —Messiah. Through the ages, Jews have looked forward to a time of peace and plenty in the future, when all nations will worship God. The Mashiaḥ will lead all people to this future time. While we are enjoying our family Ḥanukkah Minhagim, it is nice to think about a happy time in the future for all people.

REVIEW IT

1. Why are pancakes and doughnuts traditional Ḥanukkah foods?

2. Explain how the Minhag of playing dreidel can help you think of a happy future for the whole world.

3. What is your favorite Ḥanukkah Minhag?

HAVE YOU HEARD?

Dreidel is a Yiddish word from the German word meaning "to turn." In Hebrew, a dreidel or top is called סְבִיבוֹן, from the Hebrew word "to turn." The object of the game is to win the "pot" of coins, raisins, nuts, or other small items placed in front of the players. In Yiddish-speaking Jewish communities, according to Minhag, each letter on the dreidel stood not only for a Hebrew word in the sentence "a great miracle happened there" but also for a Yiddish word that gives instructions to each player. At your turn, if the dreidel fell on nun, you won *nichts*, or nothing. If it fell on gimmel, you won *ganz*—all the coins. If it fell on hay, you won *halb*, or half. If it fell on shin, you were required to *shtel*, or place your coins in the middle.

מִצְוָה

MITZVAH
mits · vä′

Mitzvah, which means "commandment," comes from the Hebrew word meaning "to command." But very often we use the word to mean an act of kindness or a good deed.

Mitzvot are their own reward.

CHAPTER TEN

According to Jewish tradition, there are 613 Mitzvot (מִצְוֹת, the plural of Mitzvah) in the Torah. The Talmud divides these into 365 Mitzvot that tell us *what not* to do (for example, "You shall not kill") and 248 that tell us *what* to do (for example, "Honor your father and mother"). The Talmud gives us a convenient way to remember the two numbers: the 365 negative Mitzvot equal the number of days in a year, while the 248 positive Mitzvot equal the number of parts of the human body.

We today are less certain than the rabbis of the Talmud were about how to calculate the exact number of Mitzvot. But there are some things we do know for sure. Like "Torah," "Mitzvah" is one of the most important words in the Jewish vocabulary. Many Jews have enjoyed performing Mitzvot so much, they have been willing to go beyond the letter of the law.

One religious Jew got so much joy out of every Mitzvah he performed that he couldn't understand why anyone should be wicked. After all, thought the Jew, the only reason the wicked perform their evil deeds is that they expect to get pleasure from them. If only the wicked would try performing Mitzvot instead! They would soon realize that nothing can give anyone as much pleasure as a Mitzvah. Then, purely in order to increase their pleasure, they would give up their wicked ways and become religious people instead!

In this chapter you will learn why, according to tradition, God revealed neither the reason nor the reward for most Mitzvot. You will also learn why some Jews have considered the Mitzvot as their best friend.

◁ Our ancestors had many ways of remembering the number of Mitzvot. According to one tradition, there are exactly as many seeds in the pomegranate as there are Mitzvot in the Torah—613.

CHAPTER SUMMARY

Lesson 1: According to Jewish tradition, the true reward for doing a Mitzvah is the privilege of doing another.

Lesson 2: Fables about the friendship of Mitzvot show just how important Jews have considered Mitzvot.

Mitzvot for their own sake

Antigonus of Socho used to say, "Don't be like servants who do what their master asks them to because they hope to get a reward for obeying. Be instead like servants who do their master's bidding without expecting any reward." Read on to find out what this statement has to do with fulfilling Mitzvot, and ask yourself:

Why doesn't the Torah specify either the reason behind most Mitzvot or the reward for them?

DOING A MITZVAH FOR ITS OWN SAKE

Even though God did not indicate the reason for most of the Mitzvot or the reward for fulfilling them, our people accepted the Torah without asking questions. Our ancestors took pride in having done so. They believed that all the Mitzvot, whether major or minor, were commanded by God.

Have you ever tried to excuse your failure to live up to a family rule by saying that the reason behind it could never apply to you? Say, for example, your parents forbid you to cook if you are alone in the house, for fear that you will burn yourself by mistake. But one day you are home alone and feel like eating instant oatmeal. You convince yourself that you could never burn yourself while making your snack. So you break the rule, only to find that you do burn yourself while pouring boiling water into the bowl. Maybe you weren't as wise as you thought.

The rabbis of the Talmud understood how people sometimes try to talk themselves out of rules whose purpose they do know. The rabbis used this understanding to explain why the Torah does not give reasons for most Mitzvot. In a similar way, the rabbis of the Midrash used another human tendency to explain why the Torah does not list the rewards for the different Mitzvot. If you get paid different amounts of money for doing certain household chores, you may be able to guess what their explanation was. If you are in a hurry some days, which chores are you more likely to fail to complete?

SEE FOR YOURSELF

Antigonus (an • tig'ə • nəs) of Socho was a Jewish teacher of the second century B.C.E.; his warning to do Mitzvot for their own sake and not just for a reward is found in Pirke Avot 1:3. You can read the story of the three gardeners in Deuteronomy Rabbah 6:2. Rabbi Yehudah HaNasi's saying about carefully observing all the Mitzvot, whether they seem major or minor, appears at Pirke Avot 2:1.

The Midrash tells this story: One day, a king hired three gardeners to tend three different trees on his property. Each gardener chose his own tree. That night, the king called all three gardeners to him. He asked each man to tell him which tree he had worked on. The gardener who tended the pepper tree got one gold piece. The gardener who tended the white-flower tree got half a gold piece. The third gardener got 200 gold pieces for tending the olive tree.

"Why didn't you tell us from the beginning how much we would be paid for each tree?" asked the men.

"If I had done that," said the king, "would you have bothered tending the pepper tree and the white-flower tree?"

In the same way, according to Jewish tradition, God did not reveal the reward for fulfilling most of the Mitzvot. Rabbi Yehudah HaNasi used to say, "Be just as careful in doing what may seem like a minor Mitzvah as you are in doing what may seem like an important Mitzvah. You do not know what the reward for each may be."

And Ben Azzai said, "The reward of a Mitzvah is another Mitzvah." The pleasure of fulfilling one Mitzvah makes a Jew more likely to perform another.

Just as the king did not tell the three gardeners what their pay would be, so the Torah does not list the reward for each Mitzvah.

REVIEW IT

1. According to the Midrash, how are Jews like the gardeners tending the king's trees?

2. How does your approach to performing Mitzvot differ from that of our ancestors?

3. Can you think of a good deed you enjoyed doing so much you wanted to do it again?

How Mitzvot are like friends

What is there about your best friend that makes you want to spend a lot of time with him or her? You probably share many of the same interests and enjoy doing things together. You probably also know that you can rely on your friend to stick by you and to back you up if you need help. Although the idea may seem strange to us today, Jews over the centuries have considered Mitzvot so important that stories have been handed down about the friendship of Mitzvot! Read one of these stories, and ask yourself:

Why are Mitzvot the most faithful friends a Jew can have?

THE FABLE OF THE THREE FRIENDS

There was once a man who had three friends. Unfortunately, the man had the deepest feelings for the friend who loved him least. But one day he had the chance to test all three friendships. For on that day, the king summoned him to his palace.

The man was very much afraid. "Perhaps," he said to himself, "someone has spread false tales about me. If so, the king may want to punish me. I know what to do. I'll ask my best friend to come with me to the king's palace to help defend me."

The man went to the friend whom he loved best, and asked him to speak on his behalf before the king. How dis-

HAVE YOU HEARD?

Are you clear about the differences between Mitzvah, Halachah, and Minhag? Consider these examples: (1) It is a Mitzvah to keep the Sabbath holy, but Halachah tells us how to go about doing that. Minhagim for Shabbat include things like eating gefilte fish and lighting different numbers of candles. (2) It is a Mitzvah to build a Sukkah, but Halachah tells us when and how. Depending on which fruits grow at the time of Sukkot in the region your parents' parents came from, your family may have a different Minhag for decorating the Sukkah than your friends' families.

appointed the man was when his friend found some excuse not to help him out.

The man approached his second friend. "I will be glad to go with you to the palace, but I am afraid I cannot defend you before the king," said this friend.

Disappointed in his other two friends, the man now approached his third friend. Although he had never regarded this friend very highly, he decided to ask for his help anyway. "Of course I shall speak on your behalf before the king," said this friend.

Helping the poor by giving Tzedakah is one of the many Mitzvot you can do.

And so it was that the man and his truest friend went before the king. The friend testified on the man's behalf, and no harm befell him.

The fable goes on to explain what this story has to do with the Mitzvot that people do during their lives.

The king is none other than God, Who calls all people before Him when it is time for them to die.

The first friend, who did not return the man's high regard for him, is money. No matter how rich a person is, his money is of no use to him at the time of his death.

The second friend, who offered to accompany the man up to the gates of the palace but not to testify on his behalf, is his family. The members of a person's family make sure that he is buried properly, but they cannot accompany a person to the grave and beyond.

The third friend, who convinced the king of the man's innocence, is the Mitzvot he performed during his life. According to the fable, when a person dies, his Mitzvot accompany him and speak to God on his behalf. For that reason, the fable considers Mitzvot to be a Jew's truest friend.

REVIEW IT

1. In the fable, how is the third friend's friendship better even than the family's?

2. How are your values similar to and different from the values presented in the fable?

3. How can you increase the pleasure you get from performing Mitzvot?

נְבִיאִים

NEVI'IM
nə · vē · ēm′

The English translation of the Hebrew word **Nevi'im** is "prophets." Nevi'im is also the name of the second section of the Tanach. The Haftarah read after the Torah on Shabbat and festivals is always a passage from the Nevi'im. In English the word "prophet" may mean someone with magical powers who can foretell the future. In Hebrew, the word Navi (נָבִיא, the singular of Nevi'im) means someone who speaks out as a spokesman for God.

The scales stand for justice—an important value for all the Nevi'im.

CHAPTER ELEVEN

The chart on the next page lists the books that make up the Nevi'im section of the Tanach. But it is in the Torah, not in Nevi'im, that we learn about Moses, the first and greatest of the Nevi'im. The closing words of the Torah state that ever since Moses, there has not been a Navi to equal him. You may know the hymn *Yigdal*, which also says that Moses was the greatest of all Nevi'im.

In this chapter, you will read about some of the fears and concerns of the Nevi'im from the time of Moses on. You will learn some of the ideas the Nevi'im shared. You will also learn that, like many great people, the Nevi'im were sometimes reluctant to act as God's spokesmen.

CHAPTER SUMMARY

Lesson 1: The Nevi'im felt compelled to act as God's spokesmen, whether they wanted to or not.

Lesson 2: The message of the Nevi'im did not always please their listeners.

Spokesmen for God

Some of the Nevi'im came from wealthy and important families. Some were poor with no family connections. One thing the Nevi'im all had in common: they felt that God had chosen them. They had to act as God's spokesmen whether they wanted to or not. Look for an answer to this question as you read on:

How did Moses and Jeremiah show their unwillingness to speak for God?

THE NEVI'IM HAD NO CHOICE

According to the Midrash, Moses was raised in the royal household of Egypt as the adopted child of Pharaoh's daughter. When Moses grew up, he used to go out among the Hebrew slaves. Despite his royal upbringing, he felt their suffering.

◁ When God spoke to Moses from the burning bush, Moses hesitated before accepting his mission as God's spokesman.

The Nevi'im נְבִיאִים

EARLY PROPHETS נְבִיאִים רִאשׁוֹנִים

Joshua	יְהוֹשֻׁעַ
Judges	שׁוֹפְטִים
I Samuel	שְׁמוּאֵל א
II Samuel	שְׁמוּאֵל ב
I Kings	מְלָכִים א
II Kings	מְלָכִים ב

The books of the Early Prophets tell the history of our people from the entry into the Promised Land with Joshua to the destruction of Jerusalem more than 500 years later.

LATER PROPHETS נְבִיאִים אַחֲרוֹנִים

Isaiah	יְשַׁעְיָה
Jeremiah	יִרְמְיָה
Ezekiel	יְחֶזְקֵאל

The books of the Later Prophets record the attempts of different prophets to turn people back to God or to comfort them after the destruction of Jerusalem and the exile to Babylon.

THE TWELVE MINOR PROPHETS תְּרֵי־עָשָׂר

Hosea	הוֹשֵׁעַ
Joel	יוֹאֵל
Amos	עָמוֹס
Obadiah	עוֹבַדְיָה
Jonah	יוֹנָה
Micah	מִיכָה
Nahum	נַחוּם
Habakkuk	חֲבַקּוּק
Zephaniah	צְפַנְיָה
Haggai	חַגַּי
Zechariah	זְכַרְיָה
Malachi	מַלְאָכִי

Among the Later Prophets are the twelve so-called Minor Prophets. These prophets are called minor not because their message is unimportant but because each of these twelve prophetic books is quite short.

HAVE YOU HEARD?

The names of the Nevi'im in Hebrew sometimes sound very different from their usual English names. If you look carefully at the chart of the Nevi'im, you can see that Jeremiah (jer • ə   mī′ə in English) sounds like yer • mə • yä′ in Hebrew. Similarly, the name Amos is ā′məs in English but ä • môs′ in Hebrew, and Ezekiel is i • zē′kē • əl in English but yə • ḥez • kāl′ in Hebrew. You know, of course, the Hebrew name of Moses, מֹשֶׁה.

One day, Moses saw an Egyptian beating one of the Hebrew slaves. To save the slave, Moses killed the Egyptian and buried the body in the sand. But two Hebrews told Pharaoh what had happened. Moses then fled to the land of Midian, where, as you may recall, he became a shepherd.

As Moses was minding the flock one day, he saw an amazing sight: a bush that was not being burnt up even though it was on fire. As he looked at the burning bush, God's voice spoke to him:

"Moses, you shall go to Pharaoh. You shall demand freedom for My people. And you shall bring My people out of Egypt."

Moses was not eager to accept this task. "But who am I," he asked, "that I should bring the Israelites out of Egypt?"

God answered, "I am with you. You must go."

But Moses still hesitated. "But I do not speak clearly. Pharaoh will never listen to me. The people will never follow me."

God assured Moses: "With My help, you will have no trouble with your speech."

But still Moses did not want to accept the mission. "Please, God," he said, "choose someone else."

God now grew angry at Moses. "Your brother Aaron speaks well. He will assist you. But you must go and do My bidding."

Moses now knew that he had no choice. He had to act as God's spokesman.

Many years later, God called on Jeremiah to act as His spokesman. This time the Navi's task was to tell the people that if they did not return to God, the Jewish state would fall.

Like Moses, Jeremiah was not eager to become a Navi. Jeremiah pleaded with God, "I am only a child. I do not know how to speak."

But God told Jeremiah not to worry. "Don't call yourself a child. You will say whatever I inspire you to say. Do not be afraid. I am with you."

The Nevi'im had no choice about whether to accept God's calling. God told the Navi Ezekiel, "I am sending you to the Israelites. You must speak My words to them, whether they listen or not." And the Navi Amos said, "Just as when a lion roars, everyone is frightened, shall God call and the Navi not answer?"

REVIEW IT

1. Name three things that Moses and Jeremiah had in common.

2. Name one major difference between the assignments of Moses and Jeremiah.

What the Nevi'im spoke out about

The Ten Commandments, which Moses presented to the Hebrews, teach people not only how to behave toward God but also how to behave toward each other. Like Moses, the other Nevi'im taught that God cares not only how we worship Him but also how we treat each other. As you read about what the Nevi'im demanded of the people, ask yourself:

What ideas did the Nevi'im share?

THE IMPORTANCE OF JUSTICE

At various times in our people's history, our leaders have seen a connection between our misdeeds and the tragedies that have befallen us. We may or may not accept this view today, but it was widely believed in the ancient world.

For example, Jeremiah warned the people that the Temple would be destroyed if they continued to treat each other badly. If the people did not deal fairly with one another, God would not permit them to live in the Promised Land.

The Nevi'im warned not only the people but also their rulers that injustice would lead to punishment. The Navi Nathan, for example, acted as King David's conscience. King David wanted to marry Bathsheba, who was already married to Uriah. After David arranged to have Uriah killed in battle,

This Yom Kippur scene was ▷ painted by a Polish artist, Maurycy Gottlieb, in the late nineteenth century. The passage from Isaiah read on Yom Kippur morning tells us that God is not pleased with our fasting if we do not help the needy throughout the year.

Nathan told the King that God would punish him by causing trouble within his family. And, in fact, David's favorite son Absalom led a rebellion against him.

The Nevi'im also taught that God is not happy with people who worship Him but do not treat other people properly. Speaking for God, Isaiah told the people: "Your gifts are useless. Your sacrifices disgust Me. I will not listen to your prayers until you stop your evil deeds and learn to do good ones, until you pursue justice and help those in need."

Every year, on Yom Kippur morning, when people are already feeling the effects of fasting, the Torah reading describes the rituals to be observed on Yom Kippur. The Haftarah, which comes from the Book of Isaiah, affects the meaning of the Torah portion in an interesting way. We hear that if we fast but do not help those in need, then God finds no favor in our fast. Only if we treat others fairly will God be pleased with us.

REVIEW IT

1. What did the Nevi'im say would happen if the people and their rulers did not pursue justice?

2. The Haftarah on Yom Kippur morning is especially interesting because it (a) stresses that fasting is the most important way to serve God, (b) questions the value of fasting by itself, (c) stresses the importance of justice, (d) *b* and *c*.

SEE FOR YOURSELF

The story of Moses and the burning bush is told in Exodus 3–4. You can read God's first call to Jeremiah and the Navi's first reluctant response in the Book of Jeremiah 1:4–8. In II Samuel 12 you can learn how the Navi Nathan acted as King David's conscience. The Yom Kippur morning Torah portions that discuss the rituals for the Day of Atonement are Leviticus 16:1–34 and Numbers 29:7–11; the Haftarah that follows is Isaiah 57:14–58:14.

סֵפֶר תּוֹרָה

SEFER TORAH
sā'fer tô·rä'

The **Sefer Torah** is the scroll of parchment on which the Ḥumash is written. The Torah is traditionally read in synagogue from a Sefer Torah, not from a bound volume of the Ḥumash. The text of the Sefer Torah contains only hand-written letters and has no vowels or punctuation.

Although סֵפֶר means "book," in ancient times there were no bound books of the kind we read today. Writings were put down on parchment.

Jews honor the Sefer Torah by decorating it with crowns, or rimmonim.

CHAPTER TWELVE

No object is more loved and respected by Jews than the Sefer Torah. Jews show their reverence for the Sefer Torah in many different ways. Draping the Sefer Torah in a beautiful silk mantle and adorning it with a decorated breastplate and crowns are ways of showing love and respect for the Sefer Torah. Rising when the Sefer Torah is removed from the ark and kissing it as it is carried through the sanctuary are other ways. When a Sefer Torah or any of its adornments become very worn or are in some way unfit to be used, they are not simply thrown out. Instead, they are stored in a safe place in the synagogue. After a while, they are taken to a cemetery and buried.

In this chapter, you will learn about the painstaking care with which each Sefer Torah is made. You will also learn about the special meanings that scholars have found in anything that looks unusual in the Sefer Torah, such as a letter that is larger or smaller than the others.

CHAPTER SUMMARY

Lesson 1: Every Sefer Torah is prepared by a trained scribe, who must follow certain rules.

Lesson 2: The Sefer Torah has many features that show how important it is.

Preparing a Sefer Torah

When you prepare a report for school, you should try your best to have it look neat. You should write with a sharpened pencil or with a good pen—not one that's about to run out of ink or one that smears. You should also try not to erase or cross out too many words. If all this effort should go into preparing a school assignment, you can imagine the effort that must go into preparing one of the holiest objects in Jewish life. As you read about how each Sefer Torah must be prepared, ask yourself this question:

What are some of the rules that must be followed in preparing a Sefer Torah?

◁ A Torah scribe, or Sofer, follows definite rules and uses special tools in preparing the Sefer Torah.

HOW A SOFER PREPARES A SEFER TORAH

Every Sefer Torah is prepared by a religious person who has been specifically trained for the task. This person is called a scribe, or, in Hebrew, סוֹפֵר. (The word "Sofer" is related to the word "sefer.") The Sofer is not free to be creative. He must follow tradition exactly. He may not decide, for example, to add vowels to the Sefer Torah he is writing, or to decorate the margins.

The Sofer must use certain materials. The parchment on which he writes must come from a kosher animal. The ink he uses must be black. After the Sofer has finished copying the text of the Torah, the sheets of parchment are sewn together with thread made from the muscles of a kosher animal. The connected sheets are then attached to wooden or ivory rollers.

No matter how well the Sofer knows the Torah, he may not write from memory. He must refer to a book that contains the Torah text, and pronounce each word before he writes it. Before he begins to write, he must say, "I am about to write this book as a sacred Sefer Torah." Each time he is about to write God's name, he must say, "I am writing this word as the Sacred Name."

A Sofer is very careful to write every letter clearly, so that it will not be confused with any other letter. He also takes pains to leave enough space around each letter so that it does not run into another letter.

Even the most skilled Sofer may make a mistake. When he does so, he can usually correct the problem. He can use a knife and pumice stone to remove the faulty letters from the parchment. It is forbidden, however, to erase the name of God. So if the Sofer makes a mistake in writing any of God's names, that piece of parchment may not be used in a Sefer Torah.

If a mistake is found in a Sefer Torah, or if the letters have faded, the scroll may not be used until a Sofer has corrected the problem. Skilled Sofrim (סוֹפְרִים, plural of Sofer) are needed to correct problems that have been found in Sifrei Torah (סִפְרֵי תוֹרָה, plural of Sefer Torah).

Many beautiful Torah decorations were made in Germany during the eighteenth century. Top, a jeweled Torah crown; bottom, an intricate silver breastplate.

REVIEW IT

1. Why is a Sofer not allowed to write from memory? Name at least three other rules every Sofer must follow.

2. How do these special rules help you understand the meaning of the word "reverence"?

3. Pick one thing you revere. What are some special ways in which you show your reverence for it?

Why the texts of Sifrei Torah must be alike

When Moses presented the teachings of the Torah to the Children of Israel, he said, "You will observe everything that I command you, without adding anything or taking anything away." In saying this, Moses did not mean that the Torah should not be interpreted. In fact, a traditional interpretation of this statement guides the Sofer in his work.

Since the vowels we use today were not added to Hebrew until centuries after the death of Moses, the Sofer knows he cannot add vowels to the text of the Sefer Torah. In the same way, the Sofer knows that if a letter appears larger or smaller than usual in the text from which he is copying, the Sefer Torah he prepares must also have the same large and small letters. As you read about some unusual details that are the same in all Sifrei Torah, ask yourself:

Why are some letters larger than usual in the Shema as it appears in all Sifrei Torah?

LARGE LETTERS IN THE SHEMA IN EVERY SEFER TORAH

The Shema is often called "the eternal watchword of our faith." A watchword is a word or phrase that expresses a belief or principle. When Jews say the Shema, they are expressing their belief in the Oneness of God.

SEE FOR YOURSELF

Moses' warning not to add anything to or take away anything from the Torah is given at Deuteronomy 13:1.

The picture shows the Shema as it appears in every Sefer Torah. Notice that the ayin in שְׁמַע and the dalet in אֶחָד are larger than normal.

One Midrash explains the unusually large *letter* ayin by referring to the meaning of the *word* ayin. "Ayin" (עַיִן) means "eye." As you know, the Shema says "Hear, O Israel, the Lord our God, the Lord is One." The large ayin teaches us that we should be aware of God's Oneness not only with our ears but with our eyes as well.

One Midrash explains the unusually large dalet by pointing out how much the letter dalet (ד) resembles the letter resh (ר). If you change the dalet in אֶחָד for a resh, then the new word אַחֵר means "other" or "another." If someone actually did mistake the word אַחֵר for the word אֶחָד , the whole meaning of the Shema would be denied! So one explanation for the large dalet is that it prevents us from misreading the Shema.

Our scholars have found important meanings in every unusual detail in the Sefer Torah. For that reason, the Sofer must be careful to copy each detail exactly.

REVIEW IT

1. Why doesn't a Sofer feel free to add vowels to the text of the Sefer Torah?

2. Give one example of a Midrash that explains the unusual appearance of the Shema in every Sefer Torah.

The Shema as it appears in the Sefer Torah, with the pointer showing an unusually large dalet.

עֲלִיָּה

ALIYAH
ä · li·yä′

Aliyah is the honor of being called up to the bimah to recite the blessings before and after the Torah reading.

In Hebrew, the word עֲלִיָּה means the act of going up. The word Aliyah also means the act of moving to Israel.

On Simḥat Torah, children below Bar or Bat Mitzvah age may be given a group Aliyah.

CHAPTER THIRTEEN

The photograph shows the bimah (בִּימָה) inside a synagogue sanctuary. As you can see, the bimah is on a higher level than the area where the members of the congregation sit. The Torah reading takes place at the reading desk on the bimah. When members of the congregation are honored with an Aliyah, they go from their seats up to the bimah.

In this chapter, you will learn how in traditional congregations people receive an Aliyah. You will also learn about some occasions when people receive special Aliyot (עֲלִיּוֹת, the plural of Aliyah).

CHAPTER SUMMARY

Lesson 1: A person who receives an Aliyah does so in a specific way.

Lesson 2: Special Aliyot are connected with Simḥat Torah, marriage, the birth of a child, and a young person's becoming Bar or Bat Mitzvah.

Receiving an Aliyah

Minhagim for reading the Torah vary from congregation to congregation. But for the moment, imagine that you are in a traditional synagogue on Shabbat morning. You are not yet of Bar or Bat Mitzvah age, so you know you will not be honored with your own Aliyah this morning. But you have decided that today you will pay extra attention to the Torah service, so you will know just what to do when your big day comes. As you read more about the steps you too will be expected to follow when you get an Aliyah, try to answer this question:

What is expected of a person who receives an Aliyah?

WHAT TO DO WHEN YOU GET AN ALIYAH

The Torah portion is divided into a certain number of sections, one for each person who receives an Aliyah. When you

◁ The bimah of Temple Beth Zion in Buffalo, New York. On either side of the Holy Ark are tablets showing the first letter of each of the Ten Commandments.

receive an Aliyah, you say the blessings before and after the Torah reading.

In many synagogues, the person who receives an Aliyah is called in the following fashion:

יַעֲמֹד דָּנִיֵּאל יַעֲקֹב בֶּן אַהֲרֹן דָּוִד וּדְבוֹרָה רִבְקָה, רְבִיעִי.

Will Daniel Jacob, son of Aaron David and of Deborah Rebecca, rise for the fourth Aliyah?

So you should know your own name and your parents' names in Hebrew.

After you hear your name called, you walk up to the bimah and stand to the right of the Torah reader. The reader shows you the exact place in the Torah where the reading will begin. With the end of your tallit in your right hand, you touch that exact place in the Torah. After that you kiss your tallit.

A Bat Mitzvah receives an Aliyah on her special day.

Now it is time for you to say the opening blessing over the Torah reading. You begin by saying:

בָּרְכוּ אֶת־יְיָ הַמְבֹרָךְ!

Bless the Lord Who is blessed.

The congregation then answers:

בָּרוּךְ יְיָ הַמְבֹרָךְ לְעוֹלָם וָעֶד!

Blessed be the Lord Who is blessed forever and ever.

You repeat the words the congregation has just answered. Then you say the first blessing, declaring that God gave the Torah to our people:

בָּרוּךְ אַתָּה, יְיָ אֱלֹהֵינוּ, מֶלֶךְ הָעוֹלָם, אֲשֶׁר בָּחַר־בָּנוּ מִכָּל־הָעַמִּים וְנָתַן־לָנוּ אֶת־תּוֹרָתוֹ. בָּרוּךְ אַתָּה, יְיָ, נוֹתֵן הַתּוֹרָה.

The reader and the congregation both say "Amen," and the reader begins reading from the Torah. After the section for your Aliyah is complete, you recite another blessing:

בָּרוּךְ אַתָּה, יְיָ אֱלֹהֵינוּ, מֶלֶךְ הָעוֹלָם, אֲשֶׁר נָתַן לָנוּ תּוֹרַת אֱמֶת וְחַיֵּי עוֹלָם נָטַע בְּתוֹכֵנוּ. בָּרוּךְ אַתָּה, יְיָ, נוֹתֵן הַתּוֹרָה.

In this blessing, you once again thank God for giving us the Torah. But this blessing makes two points the first blessing does not make—that the Torah teaches us the truth, and that God has "planted everlasting life in our midst." One meaning of this blessing is that by accepting the truths the Torah teaches us, we make it possible for the Jewish people to live on. Can you think of other meanings?

You have now finished your part, but to show that you are not anxious to leave the Torah, you do not return to your seat right away. Instead, you remain on the bimah until the next Aliyah is completed. (You do step aside, so the person receiving the next Aliyah can stand to the Torah reader's right.) When the Aliyah following yours is over, you shake hands with everyone on the bimah. They congratulate you by saying יְיַשֶׁר כֹּחַ, "May you grow in strength." As you return to your seat, members of the congregation shake your hand and congratulate you in these same words. Some people take the long way back to their seats, once again to show how sorry they are to leave the Torah.

Children play an active role in celebrating Simḥat Torah, when we finish the last words of Deuteronomy and immediately begin reading the first words of Genesis.

REVIEW IT

1. What is the special meaning of each of the following phrases? (a) תּוֹרַת אֱמֶת , (b) חַיֵּי עוֹלָם נָטַע בְּתוֹכֵנוּ , (c) יְיַשֶׁר כֹּחַ.

2. Why don't you return to your seat as soon as your Aliyah is finished?

Special Aliyot

An Aliyah at any time is a great honor. But at certain times of the year and at certain times in your life, important occasions are marked by special Aliyot. Read on to learn about some of these special Aliyot, and ask yourself:

What holiday and which events in a person's life are honored by special Aliyot?

SPECIAL ALIYOT FOR SPECIAL OCCASIONS

During the course of every year, the entire Torah is read publicly in synagogue. Every autumn, on Simḥat Torah, we finish the last words of the Torah and immediately begin reading the first words of the Torah. Simḥat Torah is a very happy occasion. It is the one day of the year when children below Bar Mitzvah age may be given an Aliyah. No one child gets the honor. Instead, some communities observe the Minhag of calling up all the children for one Aliyah. An adult leads them in the blessings before and after the Torah reading.

Special events in a person's life, such as getting married and becoming a parent, are also honored by Aliyot. According to the Midrash, when King Solomon had the First Temple built, he ordered a special entrance for bridegrooms only. When people saw a young man go into the Temple through this entrance, they congratulated him. After the Temple was destroyed, the Minhag of giving the groom an Aliyah on the Shabbat before his wedding became popular. In some synagogues, it is also a Minhag to toss nuts, raisins, or candy at the groom as he returns to his seat. In this way, the members of the congregation wish him a sweet and fruitful marriage. The fruitfulness of the marriage is also celebrated after the birth of a child, when an Aliyah is given to the parents.

On the Shabbat when you become Bar or Bat Mitzvah, both you and your parents will be honored with Aliyot. In most congregations, you will receive the Maftir (מַפְטִיר) Aliyah. "Maftir" is related to the word "Haftarah." Just as הַפְטָרָה means "conclusion," מַפְטִיר means the person who concludes the Torah service by chanting the concluding verses of the Torah portion as well as the entire Haftarah. !יִישַׁר כֹּחַ

REVIEW IT

1. On what special occasion can a child below Bar or Bat Mitzvah age be honored with an Aliyah?

2. Why do you think the Bar or Bat Mitzvah receives the last Aliyah?

עֲשֶׂרֶת הַדִבְּרוֹת

ASERET HADIBROT
ä · se′ret hä · dib · rôt′

Aseret HaDibrot is Hebrew for the Ten Commandments. "Aseret" comes from the Hebrew word for ten, and "Dibrot" means "statements." These statements include the most important principles of Jewish tradition.

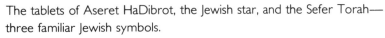

The tablets of Aseret HaDibrot, the Jewish star, and the Sefer Torah—three familiar Jewish symbols.

CHAPTER FOURTEEN

When you think of artistic symbols that convey the Jewish heritage, what comes to mind? Probably the Jewish star, the Sefer Torah, and the two tablets on which Aseret HaDibrot were engraved are among the first things you think of.

In this chapter you will learn how the first and fourth commandments are different from the other commandments. You will also discover that Judaism considers the fifth commandment to honor our parents just as important as honoring God. The final section explains how the last five commandments are related to one another.

CHAPTER SUMMARY

Lesson 1: The first commandment teaches us to be free, while the fourth is the only commandment that deals with a specific ritual.

Lesson 2: Honoring our parents is as important as honoring God.

Lesson 3: Coveting may lead to telling lies about another person, stealing someone's property, taking someone's husband or wife, and even to murder.

◁ Jewish artists have shown the two tablets of Aseret HaDibrot in many colorful ways. On this linen, an artist has painted the Hebrew letters that stand for each number of the Ten Commandments from alef (one) through yad (ten). For another way of showing Aseret HaDibrot, see page 90.

Freedom and joy

Many aspects of Aseret HaDibrot have intrigued rabbis and scholars throughout the ages. One unusual aspect is that the first commandment does not seem to be a commandment at all. Another is that the fourth commandment is the only one that deals with a specific ritual. As you read about the first and fourth commandments, ask yourself:

(a) What makes the first commandment a commandment?
(b) How is the commandment to keep and remember Shabbat only the first step in our observance?

GOD BROUGHT FREEDOM TO THE PEOPLE OF ISRAEL

Except for the first of Aseret HaDibrot, each of the Ten Commandments instructs us to do or to refrain from doing
something specific. But the first commandment only says,
"I am the Lord your God, Who brought you out of the land
of Egypt, out of the house of bondage." What, then, is the
commandment?

The commandment is to be free. Notice that God does
not describe Himself as the God Who created the universe,
although He is that, too. Instead, He describes Himself as a
God of freedom. We must imitate Him by committing ourselves to freedom for all people. Because we remember our
past as slaves, we try to improve conditions for other people
who are oppressed.

The Torah says that God's writing was engraved on Aseret HaDibrot. The Hebrew word for engraved is חָרוּת, which
is very close to the Hebrew word for freedom, חֵרוּת. If we
substitute the word חֵרוּת, we read, "freedom was on the
tablets."

SHABBAT JOY

Only the fourth commandment, to keep and remember
Shabbat, deals with the laws of a specific observance. The
other commandments deal with general moral behavior.

While Jews are supposed to observe all the Mitzvot with
joy, observing Shabbat has always been the most delightful
of all the commandments. It also reminds us of many Jewish values and practices. Traditional Jews look forward to the
coming of Shabbat so eagerly, and try to make their observance so splendid, that they speak of honoring the Shabbat
Bride or the Shabbat Queen. Tourists in Jerusalem today are
often told the story of the pious Jew who, on Sunday morning, sighs and says, "Only six more days to go."

An Aggadah is told about Rabbi Joshua ben Ḥananiah.
One Friday night, the rabbi invited the Emperor to share his
Shabbat meal. Before taking a single bite, the Emperor asked
his host to give him some of the spice that gave the rabbi's
Shabbat meal such a wonderful smell.

One way we can follow the fourth commandment to keep and remember Shabbat is by the Havdalah ceremony. Of the three Havdalah spice-boxes shown, the most unusual is the bird-shaped one at the lower left. It was crafted in Russia during the nineteenth century from silver with precious stones.

Rabbi Joshua said to the Emperor, "The spice is Shabbat itself. The wonderful odor comes from the delight we take in preparing for the Shabbat observance. There is no way I can give you any of the spice, but you may find some for yourself if only you choose to observe Shabbat."

REVIEW IT

1. How does the first commandment remind us of the importance of freedom?

2. Think of three things you and your family might do to enrich your observance of the fourth commandment.

Honoring parents

You may have noticed that God is often referred to in the Bible and in our prayers as "our Father." But did you know that Jewish tradition considers the respect we owe our own parents just as important as the respect we owe God? As you read on, look for an answer to this question:

How is the fifth commandment —"Honor your father and mother"—related to the third commandment —"Do not use God's name improperly"?

HONORING GOD AND PARENTS WITH THE PROPER ATTITUDE

In honoring our parents and in honoring God, what matters is how kind we are, not whether we give expensive gifts. The Talmud makes this point by offering an extreme example of two sons. One displeased God even though he gave his father rich food to eat. The other son pleased God even though he sent his father out to work.

The first son was a rich man who ordered his servants to give his father plump chickens to eat and wine to drink. But when his father tried to have a conversation with him, the son answered, "Be quiet, old man. Even the dogs are quiet while they eat." Obviously, this son didn't know what true generosity or true honor meant.

The second son was a poor man who supported his family, including his father, by grinding grain at a mill. One day, Roman soldiers came to the family and demanded that either the father or the son leave the mill and work as a forced laborer. The son turned to his father and said, "Father, you take my place at the mill so the family will have food to eat. The soldiers will surely use their whips on the laborers. To spare you that pain, I will go with them."

Kindliness means more than gifts when it comes to honoring God, too. As the Nevi'im said again and again, God would be angry with the people, no matter how lavish their burnt offerings, unless they acted properly. Jeremiah, for example, reported these words of God: "Of what value to Me is the incense that comes from Sheba, and the sweet cane from a distant land? I do not desire your burnt offerings, and your sacrifices do not please Me."

REVIEW IT

1. Why was God displeased with the son who gave his father plump chickens to eat and wine to drink?

2. Why did the people's sacrifices not please God in the days of Jeremiah?

The last five commandments

The last five commandments seem to deal only with a person's behavior toward other people. But since all people are God's children, by violating any one of the last five commandments, we also may be said to sin against God. As you read more about these five commandments, ask yourself:

How may breaking the tenth commandment lead to violations of other commandments?

SEE FOR YOURSELF

You can read the story of Rabbi Joshua and the Shabbat spice in the Talmud at Shabbat 119a. The tale of the covetous King Ahab and his wicked Queen Jezebel is found in I Kings 21:1–24.

COVETING LEADS TO GREATER SINS

First, let us review the last five commandments: do not commit murder, do not take another person's husband or wife, do not steal, do not tell lies about anyone, do not covet. To covet something means to want it very, very much, even though it belongs to someone else. Unfortunately, coveting what belongs to someone else can lead a person to violate other commandments.

Right next to King Ahab's palace was the vineyard of a man called Naboth. Ahab coveted the vineyard. He asked Naboth if he could buy the vineyard from him or exchange it for an even better one. But Naboth refused to give up the vineyard he had inherited from his ancestors.

Ahab's wife Jezebel saw how unhappy the King was. She planned a scheme to get Ahab the vineyard he coveted. Jezebel found two men who agreed to tell lies about Naboth. The men said Naboth was guilty of cursing God and the King. Because of this false testimony, Naboth was convicted and put to death. Ahab then took Naboth's vineyard, where he was met by the Navi Elijah. Elijah told Ahab God's message: "Have you killed and also taken possession?" God saw that Ahab's coveting led to lying, murder, and stealing.

In a similar way, King David's coveting led to several sins. One evening David stood on his palace rooftop. On a nearby roof he saw a beautiful woman, Bathsheba. You may recall

King David's sin in coveting the beautiful Bathsheba led to the further sins of murder and stealing another man's wife.

that when he learned that Bathsheba was already the wife of Uriah, David had Uriah sent to the battlefront. (He hoped that Uriah would soon be killed.) After Uriah fell in battle, David took Bathsheba as his wife.

You may also recall how the Navi Nathan acted as King David's conscience. Nathan told David a story about a man with many sheep who stole from a man with only one sheep. The Navi made David understand the comparison to the King's own situation. In this way, Nathan made David see how displeased God was with David's sins of coveting, murder, and stealing another man's wife.

REVIEW IT

1. Which commandments were violated in the story of Ahab and Naboth? Which in the story of David and Uriah?

2. How was David like a man with many sheep stealing from a man with only one sheep?

THE TEN COMMANDMENTS

1. I am the Lord your God, Who brought you out of the land of Egypt.
2. Do not have any gods before Me, and do not pray to any images.
3. Do not use God's name improperly.
4. Observe and remember Shabbat to keep it holy.
5. Honor your father and mother.
6. Do not murder.
7. Do not take another person's husband or wife.
8. Do not steal.
9. Do not tell lies.
10. Do not covet.

פָּרָשַׁת הַשָׁבוּעַ

PARASHAT HASHAVUA
pä · rä · shät′ hä · shä · vo͞o′ · ə

Parashat HaShavua is the weekly Torah portion. The Ḥumash is divided into 54 of these portions, so that with special occasions included, the entire Torah is read publicly each year.

פָּרָשַׁת means "portion of," and שָׁבוּעַ means "week."

In the Ḥumash, three Hebrew pays placed next to each other signal the start of a new Parashat HaShavua.

CHAPTER FIFTEEN

In the last Parashah of the year, וְזֹאת הַבְּרָכָה, Moses blesses the tribes of Israel before his death. We read this last Parashah on Simḥat Torah, and then immediately begin the Torah again, with the first Parashah, בְּרֵאשִׁית. The following Shabbat, בְּרֵאשִׁית is read again as Parashat HaShavua. Before the name of each Parashah in the Ḥumash, the Hebrew letter פ appears three times. The triple פ indicates the beginning of a new Parashat HaShavua.

In traditional synagogues, after the complete Parashat HaShavua is read on Shabbat morning, ten verses from the next week's Parashah are read during the afternoon services. These same verses are read again during morning services on Monday and Thursday. Then the entire Parashah is read on Shabbat morning.

The practice of reading the Torah publicly three days a week is very old. In this chapter, you will learn an Aggadah that explains why Moses felt three days should never go by without a public reading from the Torah. You will also learn the role Ezra the scribe played in instituting this practice.

CHAPTER SUMMARY

Lesson 1: Torah is often compared to water.

Lesson 2: Ezra the scribe instituted the practice of reading from the Torah publicly and regularly.

Comparing Torah to water

The Midrash often compares Torah to water. Just as water is present everywhere on earth, so is Torah. Just as water is necessary for life, so is Torah. Just as water revives a person, so does Torah. Just as water cleanses a person, so does Torah. The comparison between Torah and water helps explain why traditional congregations read the Torah publicly on Monday, Thursday, and Saturday. As you read on, look for an answer to this question:

How does Aggadah explain the public reading of the Torah on Monday, Thursday, and Saturday?

Instead of reading the whole Torah in a year, from one Simḥat Torah to the next, some congregations read the entire Torah over a three-year period. This is called the triennial cycle. Each weekly Torah portion is divided into thirds, and each year one-third of the Parashat HaShavua is read each week.

◁ A rabbi in Israel helps a Bar Mitzvah find his place in the Parashat HaShavua. In keeping with Sephardic custom, the Sefer Torah is held in a decorated case.

105

READING THE TORAH ON MONDAY, THURSDAY, AND SATURDAY

A story in the Ḥumash reports that right after the Exodus from Egypt, the Children of Israel wandered in the desert for three days without water. Until God provided them with water, they complained and quarreled.

According to an Aggadah, while Moses was on Mount Sinai, becoming familiar with the teachings of the Torah, he began to understand the spiritual as well as the physical needs of the people. Just as the people needed water to quench their physical thirst, they also needed Torah to quench their spiritual thirst. Remembering what three days without water did to the people's moods, Moses decided that three days should never go by without a public reading from the Torah. In order to prevent that from happening, the Torah would have to be read three times a week.

The Aggadah also explains the choice of Monday, Thursday, and Saturday. Careful calculation indicated that it was on a Thursday, three months after the Exodus, that Moses went up Mount Sinai to receive the Torah. Forty days later, when he returned to the people with the Torah, it must have been a Monday. So Monday and Thursday seemed good days to choose for public Torah reading. Since Saturday was Shabbat, it would be a good choice for the third day.

REVIEW IT

1. In what ways does the Midrash compare Torah to water?

2. What is one reason the Aggadah gives for reading the Torah on Monday, Thursday, and Saturday?

Ezra and weekly Torah reading

By the time the First Temple was destroyed and the Jews were taken as captives to Babylonia, most of them had forgotten the Torah. It took a great leader to revive the people with words of Torah. As you read about the life of Ezra, ask yourself:

What role did Ezra play in instituting the weekly Torah reading?

HAVE YOU HEARD?

Modern scholars reject the idea that Moses actually began the practice of reading the Torah publicly three times a week. The Ḥumash itself says at Deuteronomy 31:10–13 that Moses called for a public reading of the Torah once every seven *years!* So this Aggadah is probably only an interesting legend. But no one denies that the Midrash's comparison of Torah with water is a beautiful one!

Joshua lived around the year 1200 B.C.E., about two centuries before King David. Nehemiah (pronounced nē • ə • mī'ə in English and nə • ḥem • yä' in Hebrew) lived in the fifth century B.C.E. He held a high office at the Persian court and was made governor of Judah by the Persian king. Scholars are not sure whether Ezra the scribe was born before or after Nehemiah, or whether in fact the two ever met.

EZRA'S ROLE IN ESTABLISHING PARASHAT HASHAVUA

Ezra was a priest and scribe whose goal in life was to help his fellow Jews live once more according to the ways of Torah. When the King of Persia allowed him to return from Babylonia to Jerusalem, Ezra found that the Jews who had already come back from exile were not aware of the Torah's teachings.

On the first day of Rosh HaShanah, Ezra gathered all the people and read to them from the Torah. He began reading in the early morning and continued until noon. As they heard the words read to them, the people wept. Now they understood how far they had wandered from the path laid out by the Torah. Together with Nehemiah, another leader of the Jewish community, Ezra told the people not to weep but to celebrate.

On the second day of Rosh HaShanah, the people returned to study Torah with Ezra. They learned about the Sukkot holiday. That year, for the first time since the days of Joshua, the Jews celebrated the holiday by living in huts, or סֻכּוֹת .

Ezra arranged to have the Torah read publicly on three days a week—on Monday and Thursday, which were market days, as well as Shabbat.

Ezra understood that if the people were to base their lives on the Torah, they must be constantly reminded of its contents. So Ezra arranged to have the Torah read publicly three days a week. But Ezra's reasons for having the Torah read on Monday and Thursday were different from the reasons the Aggadah assigned to Moses. In Ezra's time, Monday and Thursday were market days, when many Jews would come together anyway.

Now that the people were once again observing the Torah's Mitzvot and not working on Shabbat, Ezra wanted to give them a chance to spend their Shabbat leisure usefully. Some of them were shopkeepers, who would not have time to hear the Torah read on market days. So Ezra began the practice of having the Torah read publicly on Shabbat afternoon as well. Ezra also set the number of Aliyot for the week's Torah-reading services: seven on Shabbat morning, and three on Mondays, Thursdays, and Shabbat afternoons.

According to the Talmud, if Moses had not lived first, God would have chosen Ezra to deliver the Torah to the people of Israel. In fact, just as Moses brought the Torah to the Children of Israel in the desert, Ezra restored it to the Jewish people after the return from Babylonian exile.

REVIEW IT

1. How long had it been before Ezra's time since the Jews last built sukkot for the Sukkot festival?

2. Why did Ezra choose Monday, Thursday, and Saturday for the public Torah reading?

3. Can you think of any other book you would like to read three times a week? For the rest of your life?

The Torah pointer, or yad, guides the reader through the weekly Torah portion. Use of the yad began as a way of making sure that bare hands would not touch the holy Torah.

רַשִׁ״י

RASHI
rä'shē

Rashi is the abbreviated name of Rabbi Shlomo Yitzḥaki, who wrote the most popular commentary on the Tanach and the Talmud. He lived in the Middle Ages, from 1040 to 1105.

The great scholar Rashi made his living growing grapes and making wine.

CHAPTER SIXTEEN

When people ask if you have begun to study the Torah, often they mean have you begun to study the Ḥumash, the Five Books of Moses. For many generations, students have used Ḥumashim (חוּמָשִׁים, the plural of Ḥumash) like the one shown. The top of the page gives the text of the Ḥumash itself. The bottom of the page gives the explanation of the text by Rashi. Although Rashi lived and wrote nine hundred years ago, his explanation of the Torah has remained the most popular.

This chapter will help you understand why Ḥumash with Rashi has been so popular for so long. The chapter opens with a popular legend about Rashi's life. The second section retells some of Rashi's comments on the story of Noah.

CHAPTER SUMMARY

Lesson 1: There are many legends about the life of Rashi, who is one of the most honored persons in Jewish history.

Lesson 2: Rashi's explanation of the Ḥumash has been an important part of Jewish education for centuries.

Legends about Rashi's life

Very little is known about Rashi's actual life. He was born in the city of Troyes, in northeastern France, in 1040 and died in 1105. Although he spent most of his time teaching Talmud, he made a living by growing grapes and making wine. Because Rashi's work on the Tanach and Talmud was so important, his fame grew. Soon his life became the subject of folktales. Although these tales are not completely true, the fact that they were told at all shows how important a figure Rashi had become in Jewish life. As you read one of these folktales, ask yourself:

◁ For many centuries, Rashi's explanation of the Ḥumash has deepened our understanding of Torah.

According to popular legend, what event took place a year before Rashi's birth?

RASHI AND THE PRECIOUS JEWEL

First, you should remember that Rashi's name is actually an abbreviation for Rabbi Shlomo Yitzḥaki, or in Hebrew רַבִּי שְׁלֹמֹה יִצְחָקִי. "Yitzḥaki" stands for "son of Isaac."

Before Rabbi Isaac had children, he was known as the owner of a very precious jewel. Even the Emperor himself had heard about Rabbi Isaac. For the only other jewel in the world of equal value to Rabbi Isaac's jewel was to be found in the eye of one of the Emperor's idols.

One day, the jewel in the eye of the Emperor's idol was reported missing. The Emperor immediately sent a messenger to Rabbi Isaac. The messenger assured Rabbi Isaac that the Emperor would pay him whatever price he wanted for the jewel. The Emperor was that anxious to have his favorite idol whole again.

Now, Rabbi Isaac was not concerned about the money the Emperor offered. Nor did he worry so much about having to give up the jewel. What did bother him was that by turning over the jewel to the Emperor, he would be furthering the worship of idols. How was he going to avoid that fate?

As he boarded the ship that would bring him closer to the Emperor's court, Rabbi Isaac immediately saw his way out of the problem. After the passengers had settled in for the journey, many of them went on deck. Rabbi Isaac, too, went on deck, taking the jewel with him.

Several passengers, seeing what was in Rabbi Isaac's hand, clustered around him. As Rabbi Isaac showed it to them, he held the jewel out as if to place it in the hand of one of its admirers. Then, as if by accident, Rabbi Isaac let the jewel fall into the sea.

At once, Rabbi Isaac put on a show of mourning. "Woe is me," he cried, "I have lost all my wealth. Worse still, I was on my way to sell this jewel to the Emperor, who would have been grateful to me forever. Now all my hopes lie with that jewel on the bottom of the sea."

The passengers, of course, comforted Rabbi Isaac. And when the ship docked and was met by the Emperor's agent, the passengers reported the "accident" that had taken place.

WHAT TIME IS IT?

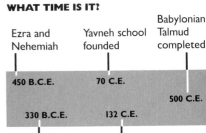

Ezra and Nehemiah	Yavneh school founded	Babylonian Talmud completed
450 B.C.E.	70 C.E.	
		500 C.E.
330 B.C.E.	132 C.E.	
Alexander the Great	Death of Akiba	

Rabbi Isaac's reward for not selling his jewel to the idol-worshiping Emperor was a "jewel" far more precious—the son we know as Rashi.

The Emperor was terribly disappointed, but he brought no charges against Rabbi Isaac. Instead, he said, "Look what bad luck that Jew had. He would have received so much gold for that jewel."

So Rabbi Isaac boarded the next ship back to his home. This time, he was met by none other than the prophet Elijah. (Remember, you're reading a folktale.) Elijah said to him, "God understands that you let the jewel slip through your fingers in order to please Him. As your reward, in a year's time, your wife will bear you a son. This son will be a jewel more precious than any other in the whole world."

And so (the story concludes), exactly a year later, Shlomo, whom we know now as Rashi, was born. There has never been a jewel to equal the value of that man, who wrote a commentary on the Tanach and the Talmud.

REVIEW IT

1. Do you think Rabbi Isaac did the right thing in causing the "accident" and then pretending to mourn?

2. Can you think of other people, either real or from stories, who are so special that we create legends about them?

Studying Ḥumash with Rashi

Rashi's explanation of the Ḥumash has always been considered very important. In fact, the first Hebrew book ever printed was Rashi's explanation of the Ḥumash *without* the Ḥumash itself! As you learn some of Rashi's explanations of the Ḥumash, ask yourself:

How do Rashi's comments help us understand the story of Noah and the flood?

RASHI'S EXPLANATIONS OF THE FLOOD STORY

Rashi's explanations of the story of Noah are typical of his method. Rashi showed that no word in the Ḥumash can be taken lightly. He often based his comments on material

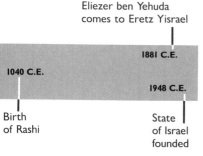

Eliezer ben Yehuda comes to Eretz Yisrael

1881 C.E.

1040 C.E.

1948 C.E.

Birth of Rashi

State of Israel founded

from the earlier rabbis of the Midrash. He also used his common sense and experience in the world of business to help draw out lessons from the Ḥumash.

Rashi used an old Aggadah to explain why God gave Noah such complicated instructions on how to make the ark. God wanted Noah to be busy building the ark for 120 years so that the wicked people among whom he lived would ask, "What are you doing?" When Noah answered, "God will soon bring a flood upon the world to punish the people for their wickedness," perhaps the wicked would mend their ways.

Rashi wondered why the Ḥumash sometimes used the simple word "rain" for the flood that lasted for forty days. He explained that the flood began as gentle rains, so that if the wicked people repented, the rain would be a blessing. But later, when God saw that the people did not repent, God turned the rain into a flood.

Noah's story opens with a description of him as a "perfectly righteous" man. Later, God told Noah that he and his family would be saved from the flood because Noah was a "righteous" man. Rashi wondered about the difference between the two descriptions. He explained: "From this we learn something about good manners, that it is proper when speaking to a man to give him only some of the praise he deserves. When he is not listening, it is proper to give him all the praise he deserves." (This explanation, too, was based on an older Midrash.)

You can see some of the ways in which Rashi's comments enrich our understanding of the Ḥumash. Rashi pointed out a basic Jewish belief, that God punishes only after giving people a chance to change for the better.

HAVE YOU HEARD?

When Rashi's explanation of the Ḥumash was first printed, the printer used the type of script then used by the Jews of Spain. Since then, this script has become associated with Rashi. It is now called "Rashi script."

SEE FOR YOURSELF

The whole story of Noah and the flood is told in Genesis 6—9.

REVIEW IT

1. How does Rashi's explanation of the Noah story show the importance of repentance in Judaism?

2. Where in the Noah story does Rashi find a lesson about good manners?

תּוֹרָה

TORAH
tô · rä′

All the Jewish beliefs, practices, and writings that have been handed down through the centuries are considered **Torah.**

The word "Torah" comes from the Hebrew word that means both "to shoot" and "to teach." So Torah actually means "guidance" or "instruction" and suggests "aiming." Everything that can teach us how to live properly may be considered Torah.

An elaborately decorated Torah pointer.

CHAPTER SEVENTEEN

What is Torah? You know that the richly adorned scroll shown in the photograph is a Sefer Torah. It contains the books of the Ḥumash. (Often people use the word "Torah" to mean the Ḥumash.) When you go to Shabbat services, a Sefer Torah like this one is removed from the ark, and portions of it are read. Many of the Bible stories you have been learning since childhood are based on the words found in the Sefer Torah. In the Torah we learn how God created the world, how He brought a great flood upon the surface of the earth, how He led the Jewish people out of slavery in Egypt, and how He gave us the Ten Commandments. In the Torah we also read about Adam and Eve, about Noah, about Abraham, Isaac, and Jacob, about Joseph, and about Moses. The Sefer Torah contains the story of the Jewish people until the time of Moses' death.

Other familiar Bible stories and biblical heroes and heroines do not appear in the Sefer Torah. King David and Queen Esther are famous biblical characters whose names do not appear in the Sefer Torah. We read about them in the books of the Nevi'im and in the Ketuvim. These books are also considered Torah, even though they are not found in the Sefer Torah.

So Torah means more than just the contents of the Sefer Torah. But it also means more than just what is in the Bible. Over the ages, Jews have lived under different conditions. To fit the times, our rabbis have based Halachah on the teachings of the Bible, and Minhagim have kept the spirit of the Bible. Torah includes the Halachah and many practices that are based on the Bible but not found in it.

But our definition of Torah is still not complete. "Torah" means "guidance" or "instruction." We can receive guidance from Bible stories and from laws and customs. But we can also be instructed by learning about the lives of wise men and women who lived after the days of the Bible. The very lives of these people are Torah, too.

One of these wise men once said that the purpose of Torah is for every person to become a Torah. He meant that by studying Bible, Aggadah, Halachah, and Minhagim, each of us can get the guidance we need to lead a good life. In turn, our lives can help guide others to lead a good life.

◁ The ornaments for this richly dressed Sefer Torah were made in Germany during the eighteenth century. The chaf and tav stand for כֶּתֶר תּוֹרָה, "crown of Torah."

In this chapter you will read some stories about Torah. The first story explains the important role children played in God's decision to give the Torah to the Jewish people. The second story teaches that Jews without the Torah are like fish out of water. The final stories in the chapter develop the idea that Torah should not be used for selfish purposes.

CHAPTER SUMMARY

Lesson 1: God would not have given the Jews the Torah if they had not pledged to teach it to their children.

Lesson 2: Just as fish cannot live for long outside of water, so the Jewish people cannot survive for long without the Torah.

Children and the giving of the Torah

Imagine that you and some friends wanted to give a party in a rented hall. The landlord would probably insist that your parents pay the rent in advance. Without your parents' pledge, you probably wouldn't be allowed to rent the hall. Children are used to having their parents back them up so they can get what they want. But when it came to the giving of the Torah, the situation was reversed. Look for the answer to this question as you read about the giving of the Torah:

What role did children play in God's decision to give the Torah to the Israelites?

Baking a Torah cake is an unusually tasty way of honoring the Torah.

CHILDREN AS PLEDGES FOR THE TORAH

God was about to give the Torah to the Israelites. They were very eager to receive the Torah's guidance. Then God said to them, "Before I give you the Torah, I need from you some pledge that you will follow the way of life the Torah teaches."

The Israelites replied, "Let our ancestors Abraham, Isaac, and Jacob be our pledges."

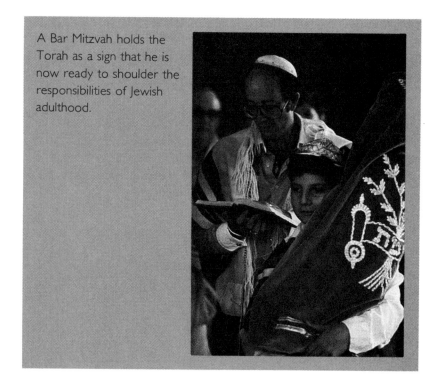

A Bar Mitzvah holds the Torah as a sign that he is now ready to shoulder the responsibilities of Jewish adulthood.

SEE FOR YOURSELF

Were you surprised to hear that God rejected the Israelites' offer of Abraham, Isaac, and Jacob as pledges for the Torah? God's complaint about Abraham is based on Genesis 15:8. Isaac's preference for Esau over Jacob is shown in Genesis 27. Finally, in discussing why God may have been dissatisfied with Jacob, the rabbis pointed to Isaiah 40:27.

Much to their surprise, God was not satisfied with this offer. "Your ancestors will not do as a pledge. Abraham doubted Me when I told him his descendants would occupy the Promised Land. Isaac preferred Esau to Jacob, even though only Jacob followed the way of Torah. Jacob himself complained that I was not concerned enough about his problems."

The Israelites thought and thought. "Let our future leaders and prophets be our pledges," they said.

Once again, God was not satisfied with their offer. "Some of your future leaders will rebel against Me. Some of your future prophets will follow false gods. You will have to come up with a better pledge before I can agree to give you the Torah."

One wise Israelite spoke to the others. "God is offering us His most precious possession, the Torah. As a pledge, let us offer Him our most precious possession—our children."

The other Israelites saw how wise this man's words were. They said to God, "We offer you our children as our pledges. If you give us the Torah, we promise to teach it to our children. They will teach it to their children. Because we will always be teaching and learning Torah, we will always remember it. And our children will make sure we follow the ways of Torah that we teach."

"This pledge I accept," said God to the Israelites. "I shall now give you the Torah. As long as you follow its teachings, I shall be with you and with your children."

REVIEW IT

1. Why did God turn down the Israelites' first two offers of pledges? Why weren't these offers good enough?

2. Why did God accept the offer of children as pledges?

3. In what way does this story show the importance of children?

The Torah is essential to Jewish life

According to the words of a famous Hebrew song, "The land of Israel without the Torah is like a body without a soul." The following story teaches that without the Torah, the people of

"Just as there is no life for the fish outside of water," Rabbi Akiba said, "so there is no life for the Jewish people without the Torah."

Israel would be lifeless, too. Torah is more than a way of life. It is a necessity of life. When you finish reading the story, you should be able to answer this question:

What animal fable did Rabbi Akiba tell to explain why he risked his life to teach Torah?

HAVE YOU HEARD?

Rabbi Akiba continued to hold Torah-study classes until he was arrested by the Romans in 132 C.E. Even in his prison cell he continued to teach Torah to visitors and to his fellow prisoners. His faith in Torah held firm even when he was tortured by the Romans. He died with the words of the Shema on his lips.

THE FOX AND THE FISH

In the time of Rabbi Akiba, the Roman Emperor ruled the land of Israel. The Emperor forbade the Jews to follow their religion. Jews were forbidden to study and teach Torah on pain of death.

All the same, Rabbi Akiba continued to hold Torah-study classes. A man once interrupted one of Rabbi Akiba's classes to ask him this question: "Rabbi, aren't you afraid of what the Romans will do to you if you continue to hold these Torah-study classes? If you value your life, why don't you simply follow the Romans' rules?"

Rabbi Akiba didn't answer the man directly. Instead, he told him the following fable.

Once upon a time, a hungry fox came to a stream. He hoped to fill his belly by outsmarting the fish swimming in the stream.

"Fish!" said the fox. "I have some important news for you. On my way through the forest just now, I saw some men headed for this stream. They are carrying nets. Obviously, they mean to catch you. But I can save you from this threat. If only you will come out of the water, I will carry you away from danger."

The fox stood by the bank of the stream licking his lips, thinking about the fine meal he would soon enjoy. Imagine his disappointment when the fish swam away from him!

"You have a reputation for being cunning, Mr. Fox," said the fish, "but really you're very foolish. As long as we're in the stream, we have a chance to avoid your clutches as well as the fishermen's nets. But as soon as we leave our watery home, we lose all hope of life."

His fable finished, Rabbi Akiba noticed that the man who had asked him the question looked puzzled. So Rabbi Akiba explained the point of the fable: "Just as there is no life for fish outside of water, so there is no life for the Jewish people without the Torah. Our lives may be in danger now while we study the Torah. But Torah is the very essence of our lives. If we stop studying it, there can be no life for us at all."

REVIEW IT

1. As you may recall, the Midrash often compares Torah to water. In this story, how is Torah like water?

2. How was Torah dangerous to Rabbi Akiba? How does the story show his willingness to risk that danger?

3. Is Torah study dangerous to Jews anywhere in today's world? Does Torah make your own life dangerous or uncomfortable in any way?

תַּלְמוּד

TALMUD
tä l · mōōd'

The **Talmud** is a collection of Halachah and Aggadah. It has two parts, Mishnah (מִשְׁנָה), written in Leshon HaKodesh, and Gemara (גְּמָרָא), written mostly in Aramaic. There are two Talmuds: the Jerusalem or Palestinian Talmud, which contains the discussions of rabbis in the academies in Israel, and the Babylonian Talmud, which contains the discussions of rabbis from the academies in Babylonia.

The Talmud records many debates between learned teachers.

123

T he Bible can easily be bound in a single volume of normal size. But the Talmud is usually bound in twelve to forty very large volumes. The Talmud is really a sort of encyclopedia, touching on all aspects of life.

The Talmud was completed almost 1500 years ago. But the teachers whose words the Talmud records seem in many ways like the people of today. The Talmud includes many incidents from the lives of these teachers. This chapter opens with two stories about two pairs of these great teachers. The second section then gives two examples of how the Gemara adds to the Mishnah.

CHAPTER SUMMARY

Lesson 1: The Talmud contains not only laws but also interesting stories about the lives of the teachers whose words are recorded there.

Lesson 2: The Gemara explains the Mishnah from the point of view of the rabbis who lived some generations later.

The rabbis of the Talmud had everyday problems

Can you and your best friend disagree without harming your friendship? Do leaders of our country sometimes differ on important matters without losing respect for one another? The same was true of the rabbis of the Talmud. Often what we find in the Talmud are debates between two teachers. The Talmud not only records their debates but also sheds light on the relationship between each pair of teachers. Look for answers to these questions as you read on:

(a) What does the story about the non-Jew and Torah teach us about Hillel and Shammai?
(b) How did Rabbi Yoḥanan's influence change Simeon ben Lakish?

◁ A young Israeli ponders a page of Talmud.

HOW HILLEL WON A CONVERT

A non-Jew once came to Shammai with the following challenge: "I will convert to Judaism if you can teach me the entire Torah while I stand on one foot." Shammai found the request annoying. Impatiently he pushed the non-Jew away.

The non-Jew then approached Hillel. Hillel was not angry, and he did not send the man away. Instead, he converted the non-Jew by summarizing the Torah in his own words: "Don't do to your neighbor anything that you yourself find hateful." Hillel then sent the new convert off to study the Torah in detail.

Hillel and Shammai were great leaders during the period of the Mishnah. Each man was the head of an academy. Hillel's academy was known as Bet Hillel, which means "House of Hillel," and Shammai's academy was known as Bet Shammai. Generations later, the scholarly debates between the two men and between their academies remained a model for the disputes in the Gemara.

Shammai rejected the non-Jew's challenge, but Hillel won a convert through patience and wisdom.

According to the Gemara, for three years Bet Shammai and Bet Hillel disputed a single point. Each side claimed that the Halachah supported its own point of view.

Then a mysterious voice was heard. "Both sides speak the words of the living God," said the voice, "but the Halachah agrees with the rulings of Bet Hillel."

The rabbis wondered how the Halachah could be said to favor Bet Hillel if both sides spoke the words of the living God. They concluded that Bet Hillel earned this honor because of the fairness and modesty the members of that academy showed. Not only did they study the rulings of Bet Shammai in addition to their own, but they even honored the opposing view by mentioning it first.

HOW A GLADIATOR BECAME A SCHOLAR

When he was young, Simeon ben Lakish was so poor he had to drop out of school. To earn money, he became a gladiator—a fighter who fought at public shows to entertain the Romans. Only the strongest gladiators survived.

One day the great scholar Rabbi Yoḥanan was taking a bath in the Jordan River. He saw Simeon diving into the water and noticed how strong he was. Rabbi Yoḥanan said to him, "You should use your strength to study Torah."

Now, Rabbi Yoḥanan was a very handsome man. Simeon answered him by saying, "You should use your good looks to win women."

Simeon's clever answer impressed Rabbi Yoḥanan. He made Simeon the following offer: "If you give up fighting for pay and go back to your studies, you may marry my sister, who is as good-looking as I am."

As a result, Simeon ben Lakish returned to his studies and became one of the most important scholars of his day. He and his brother-in-law Rabbi Yoḥanan did not always agree as they discussed sections of the Mishnah. But Rabbi Yohanan found his debates with Rabbi Simeon very important. When Rabbi Simeon was absent, Rabbi Yoḥanan compared himself to a man trying to applaud with only one hand.

HAVE YOU HEARD?

In reading the story of Simeon ben Lakish and Rabbi Yoḥanan, you may have wondered how Rabbi Yoḥanan could have promised so quickly to let Simeon marry his sister. After all, she had never met Simeon, and Rabbi Yoḥanan didn't even ask her opinion before he made his promise. In ancient times, it was common for a father, an uncle, or a brother to arrange the marriage of any unmarried woman in the family. The rabbis accepted this practice, but they ruled that the marriage could not take place without the woman's consent.

REVIEW IT

1. Which word best describes a quality that Hillel had but Shammai lacked? (a) patience, (b) strength, (c) beauty.

2. When and why did Rabbi Yoḥanan compare himself to a man trying to applaud with only one hand?

3. Think of a friend with whom you sometimes enjoy a friendly disagreement. What is one subject the two of you enjoy arguing about?

The Gemara adds to the Mishnah

Sometimes the rabbis of the Gemara stuck very closely to the Mishnah's text. They explained passages of Mishnah by referring to history or to passages in the Bible. At other times, a topic raised in the Mishnah brought folktales, old sayings, or personal thoughts to the minds of the rabbis quoted in the Gemara. After reading this section, you should be able to answer these two questions:

(a) What does the Gemara add to the Mishnah about the punishment for injuring another person?
(b) What topic in the Mishnah leads to the Gemara's story about Alexander the Great's love of gold?

PAYMENT, NOT MUTILATION

In reviewing the Mishnah's laws about the punishment for injuring another person, the rabbis of the Gemara were puzzled. The Mishnah says that whoever injures another person must pay the injured party. But doesn't the Ḥumash teach that whoever blinds another person must be blinded as punishment?

The rabbis of the Gemara pointed to two other passages in the Ḥumash that support the ruling of the Mishnah. The first passage discusses injuries to human beings together with injuries to animals. If a person makes up for an injury done to an animal by paying money instead of by an injury to himself, argued the rabbis, it stands to reason that the

HAVE YOU HEARD?

The idea of punishing someone by mutilation (myōot·ə·lā'shun) is very ancient. You may have heard the expression "an eye for an eye, a tooth for a tooth," which comes from Exodus 21:24. Today, mutilation is no longer a part of Jewish law. But there are some countries where mutilation is still an accepted form of punishment. In these countries, a thief may be punished by having his hand cut off, and a person who takes someone else's husband or wife can be stoned to death.

person should also pay money when he injures another human being.

The second passage helps by stating that a murderer cannot "undo" his crime by paying money. This suggests that for injuries that do not result in death, a person *can* pay for his crime through money and not mutilation.

ALEXANDER THE GREAT AND OTHER PEOPLE'S PROPERTY

Studying Mishnah and Gemara is a lifelong task.

The rabbis of the Gemara were studying a section in the Mishnah. The section discusses what to do when you find an item by chance, wrapped up with a purchase you have made. The following story came to mind, and is included in the Gemara.

Alexander the Great visited King Katzya to learn about the customs of his land. While the two leaders were talking, two men came before the King. One said, "I bought a field from this man. Now I have found a treasure of gold on it. Since I bought only the field and not the treasure, I want to return the money to him. But he refuses to take it."

The second man insisted, "When I sold him the field, I sold him everything on it and in it. The treasure belongs to him, and I won't take it back."

King Katzya said to the first man, "I know how to solve your argument. Have *your* son marry *his* daughter, and let *them* have the gold."

When the men left happily, Alexander told Katzya how he would have handled the problem. "I would have put both men to death and taken the money myself."

Katzya then asked Alexander, "Are there any animals in your country?" When Alexander assured him that there were, Katzya said, "Whatever blessings God bestows on your country must be for the sake of those animals. People like you are not worthy of God's blessings."

REVIEW IT

1. The rabbis of the Talmud were able to keep the law while making it more humane for their time. Give an example.

2. Suppose you heard someone argue that the Talmud is only a book of laws. How would you prove him wrong?

תַּלְמוּד תּוֹרָה

TALMUD TORAH
tăl · mo͞od′ tô · rä′

Talmud Torah is the Mitzvah of studying and teaching Torah. The rabbis of the Talmud taught that all people should practice Talmud Torah. The expression is made up of the word תַּלְמוּד, meaning "study," and the word תּוֹרָה, meaning "teaching."

The taste of honey means a sweet start in Talmud Torah.

CHAPTER NINETEEN

The picture shows a traditional Hebrew elementary school in Eastern Europe before World War II. The woman sitting at the desk alongside these young girls is their teacher.

Over the centuries, many Jewish parents have struggled to fulfill the Mitzvah of teaching Torah to their children. But this has not always been the case. Not all parents have been equally concerned with making sure their children receive a good religious education. You may know some adults who take time to study Torah on their own or with other adults, but there are also many adults who busy themselves in other ways. Even the parents of some of the greatest rabbis of the Talmud did not provide their young children with a religious education. When these children grew up, they had to make the decision on their own to fulfill the Mitzvah of Talmud Torah.

The first part of this chapter tells a story about a Minhag aimed at making sure that a child's introduction to Talmud Torah was sweet. The second section describes how one rabbi saved Judaism by his belief in the importance of Talmud Torah. In the final section you will read about a great rabbi who did not begin his studies until he was an adult.

CHAPTER SUMMARY

Lesson 1: A child's introduction to Torah studies should be sweet.

Lesson 2: A school for teaching Torah saved Judaism.

Lesson 3: A person is never too old to start learning Torah.

◁ A Jewish girls' school in Poland before World War II. In Eastern Europe at this time, boys and girls were usually taught in separate schools—and many girls did not go to school at all.

Sweetening a child's studies

Most of us began our religious studies as young children without our parents making any special fuss. But for generations, parents held public celebrations on the day their child's Hebrew education began. Many communities observed the following Minhag: as a child entered the class-room for the first time, the teacher dropped a penny on the child's head. This act was meant to show that the angels above were rewarding the child. In other communities, the child's first lesson was covered with honey. Read on to understand the reason for this Minhag, and ask yourself:

What is the origin of the Minhag of spreading honey on a child's first lesson?

THE LEGEND OF THE HONEY

If you had ever met Simon ben Yehudah, chances are you would have found him a perfectly ordinary man. He was neither very thin nor very fat, very handsome nor very ugly, very rich nor very poor, very learned nor very ignorant. There seemed to be nothing at all unusual about him.

But the angels in heaven knew that Simon was outstanding in one way: whenever he had the opportunity, he acted with kindness. A grocer by trade, Simon would willingly give a poor customer the finest fruits and vegetables. He did so without hoping to be rewarded by God or by other people.

One day, an angel came to Simon's shop, dressed in a beggar's rags. Without waiting for his new customer to speak, Simon loaded him down with the reddest apples, the plumpest raisins, and the most fragrant oranges to be found in his shop.

After the angel returned to heaven, he called a meeting of all the angels to discuss how they could best reward Simon for his acts of kindness. Simon already had a loving wife, a healthy baby, and enough money. What could they do for him to bring him the most joy?

For a full seven days and seven nights, the angels pondered the question. Then they had an idea: they would see to it that his baby son would grow up to be a great scholar.

The angels then searched the world for the purest honey made by the best bees who had gathered nectar from the world's most beautiful flowers. Having gathered the honey, the angels waited.

This photograph was taken in an Israeli school run by the Jewish Agency as part of its Youth Aliyah program.

Time passed, and Simon's son was no longer a baby. The day came when Simon took him to school for the first time. As the boy opened his first schoolbook, a tempting smell rose from its pages and filled the classroom. The boy touched the letters on the book's first page and brought his fingers to his lips. The taste of the honey that was spread over the page was sweeter than anything he had ever known.

The boy's delight in the honey that was spread over the lesson was matched by his delight in the lesson itself. Finding all his studies as sweet as the first day of study had been, the boy grew up to be a great scholar.

In the hope that a sweet beginning in Talmud Torah would encourage their children to be scholars too, parents began the Minhag of spreading honey on the pages of their children's first lesson.

REVIEW IT

1. What do the Minhagim of dropping a penny on a school-child's head and of spreading honey on a child's first lesson have in common?

2. There is a saying about study: "If you see a student who finds his studies as hard as iron, it is because his teacher does not act in a cheerful way." How is this saying related to the Minhagim about the penny and the honey?

How a school for Torah saved Judaism

The Second Temple stood in Jerusalem for more than 500 years. While it stood, it was the center of Jewish life. The Romans' destruction of the Temple was a terrible blow to the Jews. After all, without the Temple how could they worship God according to the Torah's laws? What would happen to the sacrifices made by the priests and Levites? But because of one rabbi's understanding of the importance of Talmud Torah, the destruction of the Temple did not end Judaism. This rabbi helped change Judaism from a religion of sacrifices by priests to a religion of Torah for all Jews. As you read about Rabban Yoḥanan ben Zakkai and his school, look for an answer to this question:

Why was the school at Yavneh so important?

THE SCHOOL AT YAVNEH

Before destroying the Temple, the Roman general Vespasian gave the Jews of Jerusalem a chance to save their city and their Temple by surrendering. The leaders, however, refused.

The head of the Sanhedrin (סַנְהֶדְרִין), Rabban Yoḥanan ben Zakkai, cared more about saving Judaism than about anything else. So he, too, urged the people to save the city and the Temple by surrendering to Vespasian. But the leaders refused his request. After they had turned down his request for the third time, Rabban Yoḥanan ben Zakkai decided to take matters into his own hands. (Of course, he under-

Rabban Yoḥanan ben Zakkai faked his own death so that he could be smuggled out of Jerusalem to set up a school at Yavneh.

HAVE YOU HEARD?

"Sanhedrin"—pronounced san • hed'rin in English and sän • hed • rēn' in Hebrew—comes from a Greek word meaning "council." During Roman times, the Sanhedrin was like a combined Congress and Supreme Court of Judaism. The Sanhedrin met in Jerusalem until the Romans destroyed the city and its Temple. Then, for the next several decades, the Sanhedrin held its meetings in Yavneh, located west of Jerusalem and south of Jaffa. The students of Rabban Yoḥanan ben Zakkai at Yavneh were the first people actually to hold the title "Rabbi." Yoḥanan ben Zakkai held a special title, "Rabban"—"Our Master"—because he was the head of the Sanhedrin.

SEE FOR YOURSELF

You can read the account of how Rabban Yoḥanan ben Zakkai escaped from Jerusalem and saved Judaism at Yavneh in the Avot d'Rabbi Natan 4.

stood the leaders' unwillingness to give in to the enemy. But he felt there was no other choice.)

Now, the Jewish leaders of Jerusalem knew that many people in the city would rather surrender than fight. They knew that if they did not force the people to stay in Jerusalem, many would flee. So they refused to let anyone out.

But Rabban Yoḥanan ben Zakkai had a plan. He sent for two of his students. "Spread the rumor that I am deathly ill," he said. "Then wrap my body in cloth, and carry me out of Jerusalem as if I were dead." Everyone knew that dead bodies were not allowed to remain in Jerusalem overnight.

The plan worked perfectly. The bearers of the body were allowed out of the city. The students then carried their teacher to the Roman camp and asked to see Vespasian. Vespasian had heard reports from his spies that Yoḥanan ben Zakkai had asked the Jewish leaders to surrender. For that reason, the general thought well of the rabbi.

"What may I do for you?" asked Vespasian.

"I ask only a small favor," answered Yoḥanan ben Zakkai. "Please let me set up a school in Yavneh, where I may teach Torah to my students, say my prayers, and perform the Mitzvot."

"Certainly," said the general. He did not realize that by granting this request, he was ensuring the future of the Jewish people.

So Rabban Yoḥanan ben Zakkai left the Roman camp and founded his academy at Yavneh. After Jerusalem fell and the Temple was destroyed, Yavneh became the new center of Jewish life. Sacrifices were no longer made, but the study of Torah went on. At his school, Rabban Yoḥanan ben Zakkai trained rabbis to keep Torah alive by teaching it to the people.

REVIEW IT

1. Why did Rabban Yoḥanan ben Zakkai have himself smuggled out of Jerusalem?

2. For what two reasons was Vespasian willing to give Rabban Yoḥanan ben Zakkai what he requested?

3. How do you think Judaism would be different today if the Temple had not been destroyed?

4. Consider arguments for and against Rabban Yoḥanan ben Zakkai's going to Vespasian.

It's never too late to begin studying Torah

Studying is important for Jews—so important that some rabbis of the Talmud explained the destruction of the Second Temple as God's way of punishing the Jews for not educating their children properly. Not everyone accepts this view, but we do know of at least two men, Eliezer ben Hyrcanus and Akiba ben Joseph, who were not educated as children. Their decision to begin Talmud Torah when they were adults caused them many personal problems. Yet they became great leaders who helped the Jewish people survive the loss of Jerusalem and the Temple. Read about the struggle of Akiba ben Joseph to fulfill the Mitzvah of Talmud Torah, and ask yourself:

How does the education of Rabbi Akiba show that it is never too late to begin the study of Torah?

Three rabbis debate a Talmudic point in an early morning study session.

RABBI AKIBA, THE DONKEY, AND THE ROCK

The famous Rabbi Akiba came from a much more humble home than did Rabbi Eliezer. Eliezer's father had objected to learning, but he was a landowner. Akiba's father, Joseph, was a poor peasant who owned no land of his own and worked on a neighbor's estate. Joseph did not know how to read or write and could teach Akiba nothing except how to tend sheep.

Akiba grew up and got a job tending sheep for a rich man named Kalba Savua. Now, Kalba Savua had a lovely daughter named Rachel. Akiba admired Rachel but had no hopes of ever getting to know her. After all, why would she want to have anything to do with an ignorant shepherd like him?

HAVE YOU HEARD?

Eliezer ben Hyrcanus was one of the two students who carried the body of Rabban Yoḥanan ben Zakkai out of Jerusalem. He thus helped his great teacher found the academy at Yavneh that became the religious center of the Jews after the destruction of the

Second Temple. Joshua, who helped Eliezer carry the body, also became a great scholar. These two students of Yohanan ben Zakkai are the same Rabbi Eliezer and Rabbi Joshua whose argument on Halachah is given in the section on Halachah (pp. 13–14).

But one day, Rachel noticed Akiba as he was tending the flock. Something about him seemed exceptional to her, and she spoke to him. Although Akiba was clearly uneducated and his speech was rough, she could tell that he was a very bright man.

"How do you know so many interesting things?" she asked him.

"Whatever I know, I have learned from God's nature that surrounds me," answered Akiba.

"Then think how vast your knowledge would be if you knew Torah, too," she said. The two continued to meet, and each day she urged Akiba to give up his job and go study Torah.

"But I'm already a grown man," he said to her. "Students and teachers alike will make fun of me because I know nothing."

"Let me prove to you that you're wrong," said Rachel. "Bring me a donkey with a sore back."

Although he did not see the connection between the donkey and his own case, Akiba did what Rachel asked. When he had brought the donkey, Rachel covered the sore on its back with dirt and ointment until it looked ridiculous.

"Now let's take the donkey to market each day for a week and see what happens," she told him.

On the first day, people stared at the donkey and laughed. On the second day, fewer people noticed the donkey, but those who did laughed again. By the third day, no one laughed any more.

"What happened with the donkey will happen with you, too," said Rachel. "Go study Torah. The first day your teachers and classmates may laugh at you, but in a few days their laughter will stop and they will accept you for what you are."

Akiba agreed to study Torah. Before he left Kalba Savua's house, he and Rachel married, against her father's wishes. Rachel, too, was forced to leave her father's home. In order to support herself in her husband's absence, she cut off her hair and sold it.

Akiba's introduction to Talmud Torah was not easy. He

was very discouraged at first. One day, he went for a walk in the woods to be alone with his unhappiness. He noticed a granite boulder standing in a stream of rushing water. In the center of the boulder was a large hole the water had carved out by erosion.

All of a sudden Akiba's attitude changed. "If the rushing water can carve a hole in a hard rock," he said to himself, "then the words of Torah can find their way into my hard head."

Years later Akiba returned home, but now he was a famous rabbi. His father-in-law was proud to take him and Rachel back into his home.

Akiba said to his father-in-law, "Rachel understood that Talmud Torah is the most important Mitzvah. Without her, I would have achieved nothing. Whatever respect you pay me as a scholar belongs to Rachel as well."

REVIEW IT

1. What lesson did Akiba learn from the donkey? From the granite boulder?

2. What role do you expect Talmud Torah will play in your future?

HAVE YOU HEARD?

Today, as in ages past, the Mitzvah of Talmud Torah is being fulfilled in Jewish schools throughout the world. In the United States, famous scholars practice Talmud Torah at such great centers of Jewish learning as the Reform movement's Hebrew Union College—Jewish Institute of Religion (founded in 1875), the Conservative movement's Jewish Theological Seminary (1886), the Orthodox movement's Rabbi Isaac Elchanan Theological Seminary of Yeshiva University (1896), and the Reconstructionist Rabbinical College (1968). You, too, perform the Mitzvah of Talmud Torah as you learn Torah from this book and from your teachers.

תַּנַ"ךְ

TANACH
tä · näḥ'

The **Tanach** is the Hebrew Bible. The word is made up of the first letter of each of the Hebrew words Torah, Nevi'im, and Ketuvim. Torah (the Ḥumash), Nevi'im (Prophets), and Ketuvim (Writings) are the three main divisions of the Tanach.

The Tanach is like an entire library.

CHAPTER TWENTY

Imagine that you are looking at several volumes on a bookshelf in a Jewish home. The top line on the spine of each book says תַּנַ״ךְ. The Tanach is the Hebrew Bible. The next three lines on the books' spines list the contents of the Bible: the Torah (תּוֹרָה), or Ḥumash; the Nevi'im (נְבִיאִים), or Prophets; and the Ketuvim (כְּתוּבִים) or Writings. If you combine the first letter of each of the words תּוֹרָה, נְבִיאִים, כְּתוּבִים, you get the word תַּנַ״ךְ.

This chapter introduces you to two famous sayings about the Tanach. One saying was originally spoken in Aramaic, the other in Leshon HaKodesh. The Aramaic statement teaches that the Tanach contains everything. The Hebrew statement is a pun that teaches us never to neglect the Tanach.

CHAPTER SUMMARY

Lesson 1: The Tanach contains all the variety of life itself.

Lesson 2: A Hebrew pun teaches Jews not to neglect the Tanach.

The Tanach is as varied as life itself

The books of the Tanach touch on all aspects of life. Many sections present history, ranging from love stories to family quarrels to wars. Other sections spell out laws. In the prophetic sections, the behavior of the whole nation is judged. Some sections contain prayers, often prayers of thanks. Other parts of the Tanach offer advice on how to handle life's problems. This type of material is called wisdom literature. The Tanach is like a library. In it a reader can find something to suit any mood. Read on to see how one reader of long ago described the Tanach, and ask yourself this question:

What did Ben Bag-Bag say about the Tanach?

THE TANACH CONTAINS EVERYTHING

Different stories are told about how Yoḥanan ben Bag-Bag got his unusual name. The stories agree on one thing: Ben Bag-Bag was a convert to Judaism. He was not born into a life of Torah and Mitzvot. He chose to accept such a life.

◁ Using hand-lettered scrolls, illustrated manuscripts, printed Bibles, and today even computers, Jews have continued to make the Tanach a part of their lives.

Ben Bag-Bag's summary of the Tanach is so important that it was recorded in the Mishnah. Since the part of the Mishnah in which it appears is also reprinted in Hebrew prayerbooks, Ben Bag-Bag's words are at your fingertips whenever you go to synagogue.

Here, translated from the Aramaic, is what Ben Bag-Bag had to say about the Tanach:

> Leaf through it and then leaf through it again, for it contains everything. Look into it, and become old and gray in it. Do not move away from it, for you have no better standard of conduct than it.

REVIEW IT

1. Why is it interesting to know that Ben Bag-Bag was a convert to Judaism?

2. What did Ben Bag-Bag mean when he said "become old and gray in it"?

What a pun teaches us about the Tanach

Do you know any puns? A pun is a clever way of calling attention to the different meanings of words that sound alike. Sometimes puns may be corny. For example, you may know the old joke, "Who was bigger, Mr. Bigger or his son?" The answer is, "The son was a little Bigger." Sometimes a pun can be instructive as well as humorous. As you read on, ask yourself:

What does the other Hebrew word that sounds the same as Tanach mean, and what does the pun teach us?

A PUN TEACHES US NOT TO NEGLECT THE TANACH

Two different Hebrew words are pronounced tä • näḥ', even though they are spelled differently and mean different things. The other tanach is spelled תַּנַּח, and it means "you shall let rest."

A famous Hebrew pun plays the two sound-alike words off against each other: מִן הַתַּנַ"ךְ יָדְךָ אַל תַּנַח. The saying means, "Do not let your hand rest from the Tanach," or "Do not neglect the Tanach."

If, over the course of your lifetime, you continue to dip into the Tanach, as well as into other books of Jewish knowledge, you will continue to learn much about the Jewish way of life.

REVIEW IT

1. One reason the Tanach is not to be read through in a single sitting is its length. Can you think of at least one more reason?

2. One way of "not letting your hand rest from the Tanach" is to read the commentaries of later scholars. In this book you have learned about many of these commentaries. Can you name at least three other kinds of writings that we call "Torah"?

Schoolboys in Jerusalem study the Tanach.

GLOSSARY

in English alphabetical order

Aggadah (אַגָּדָה); literally, "story"; everything in the Talmud that is not specifically legal in content. Aggadah includes proverbs, discussions, legends, historical anecdotes, and scientific lore intended to show the way to righteous behavior.

Aliyah (עֲלִיָּה), *pl.* Aliyot (עֲלִיּוֹת); literally, "going up, ascent." 1. The honor of being called up to the synagogue platform (bimah) from which the Torah is read. 2. Pilgrimage or immigration to Israel.

Aseret HaDibrot (עֲשֶׂרֶת הַדִּבְּרוֹת); the Ten Commandments.

Gemara (גְּמָרָא); literally, "completion," from the Aramaic word meaning "to learn." Gemara is the part of the Talmud that comments on and amplifies the meaning of the Mishnah. The Jerusalem (or Palestinian) Gemara was compiled in Eretz Yisrael between 200 and 400 C.E.; the Babylonian Gemara was compiled between 200 and 500 C.E. by Jews living in Babylonia under Persian rule.

Haftarah (הַפְטָרָה); literally, "ending"; the passage from the Nevi'im that follows the Torah reading in synagogue on Shabbat and holidays.

Haggadah (הַגָּדָה); literally, "story"; the story of Passover, or the book in which it is told. See also **Aggadah**.

Halachah (הֲלָכָה); from the Hebrew word meaning "to walk." 1. Jewish law. 2. The portion of the Talmud dealing specifically with legal matters.

Humash (חוּמָשׁ), *pl.* Humashim (חוּמָשִׁים); from the Hebrew word for "five"; the Five Books of Moses, making up the first section of the Tanach.

Ketuvim (כְּתוּבִים); literally, "writings"; the third section of the Tanach, including the Book of Psalms, the Book of Proverbs, the Book of Job, the five Megillot, and other books.

Leshon HaKodesh (לְשׁוֹן הַקֹּדֶשׁ); literally, "the holy language"; Hebrew.

Maftir (מַפְטִיר); the person who concludes the Torah service by chanting the closing verses of the **Torah** portion as well as the entire **Haftarah**.

Mashiah (מָשִׁיחַ); a person anointed with holy oil; the Messiah, a savior who, according to the traditional belief, will re-establish the kingdom of Israel, thereby bringing peace, righteousness, justice, and happiness to the world.

Megillah (מְגִלָּה), *pl.* Megillot (מְגִלּוֹת); literally, "scroll." The five Megillot, all found in the **Ketuvim**, are the Song of Songs, read on Passover; the Book of Ruth, read on Shavuot; the Book of Lamentations, read on Tisha b'Av; Ecclesiastes, read on Sukkot; and the Book of Esther, read on Purim.

Mezuzah (מְזוּזָה), *pl.* Mezuzot (מְזוּזוֹת); literally, "doorpost"; a small metal or wood box containing a piece of parchment on which are written the first two paragraphs of the Shema.

Midrash (מִדְרָשׁ); literally, "investigation"; a type of rabbinic literature that explains and amplifies the Bible, often through maxims and stories.

Minhag (מִנְהָג), *pl.* Minhagim (מִנְהָגִים); a Jewish custom. Unlike **Halachah**, which is slow to change and is applicable to all Jews, Minhagim (such as the number of candles lit at home on Shabbat) may vary from place to place and even from household to household.

Mishnah (מִשְׁנָה); literally, "study"; part of the Talmud compiled by Yehudah HaNasi and his followers at Yavneh by 200 C.E.

Mitzvah (מִצְוָה), *pl.* Mitzvot (מִצְוֹת); literally, "commandment." 1. One of the 613 commandments the Ḥumash is traditionally believed to contain. 2. Any good deed or act of kindness.

Nevi'im (נְבִיאִים), *sing.* Navi (נָבִיא); literally, "spokesmen for God." 1. The Hebrew Prophets. 2. The prophetic books of the Hebrew Bible, making up the second section of the Tanach.

Parashat HaShavua (פָּרָשַׁת הַשָּׁבוּעַ); literally, "portion of the week"; the weekly **Torah** portion read in synagogue on Shabbat and special occasions.

Rashi (רַשִׁי); a short name for Rabbi Shlomo Yitzḥaki (1040−1105), author of the most popular commentary on the Tanach and Talmud.

Sefer Torah (סֵפֶר תּוֹרָה), *pl.* Sifrei Torah (סִפְרֵי תּוֹרָה); the scroll of parchment on which the Ḥumash is inscribed.

Shaddai (שַׁדַּי); Hebrew word for "Almighty." The Hebrew letters that make up "Shaddai" stand for "guardian of the doors of Israel," and every **Mezuzah** bears either the word "Shaddai" or its first Hebrew letter, shin.

Sofer (סוֹפֵר), *pl.* Sofrim (סוֹפְרִים); a **Torah** scribe.

Talmud (תַּלְמוּד); literally, "learning" or "instruction"; sacred book of Jewish practice, including the **Mishnah** and the **Gemara**. The Jerusalem (or Palestinian) Talmud contains the discussions of the rabbis in the academies of Israel (Jerusalem or Palestinian Gemara); the Babylonian Talmud contains the discussions of the rabbis of the academies in Babylonia (Babylonian Gemara).

Talmud Torah (תַּלְמוּד תּוֹרָה); literally, "study teaching." 1. The **Mitzvot** of studying and teaching **Torah**. 2. A school where **Torah** is taught, especially a Jewish grade school.

Tanach (תַּנַ"ךְ); the Hebrew Bible, comprising the **Torah** (Ḥumash), Nevi'im, and **Ketuvim**.

Torah (תּוֹרָה); literally, "guidance" or "instruction." 1. The whole of Jewish beliefs, practices, and writings. 2. The Ḥumash. 3. A **Sefer Torah**.

INDEX

Key to pronunciation: **a** as in r**a**n, S**a**bbath; **ä** as in f**a**ther, M**a**tzah; **ā** as in p**a**y, s**e**der; **e** as in l**e**t, t**e**mple; **ē** as in dr**ea**m, H**e**brew; **ə** as in **a**bout, helpf**u**l, proph**e**t; **i** as in p**i**n, M**i**tzvah; **ī** as in f**i**ve, rabb**i**; **o** as in p**o**t, h**o**stage; **ô** as in b**ou**ght, p**o**rtion; **ō** as in b**oa**t, M**o**ses; **o͞o** as in w**oo**d, Kibb**u**tz; **o͞o** as in tr**ue**, R**u**th.

ON THE COVER All illustrations by Tony Chen. Photographs: Jay M. Pasachoff (children playing with dreidel); James Nachtwey/Black Star (Torah scribe, computer console operator); Rick Friedman/Black Star (rabbi holding yad); Jewish Museum/Art Resource (Sefer Torah).